D0186915

EDWARD SAPIR

Culture, Language, and Personality

EDWARD **SAPIR**

CULTURE, LANGUAGE

AND PERSONALITY

SELECTED ESSAYS EDITED BY

David G. Mandelbaum

UNIVERSITY OF CALIFORNIA PRESS
BERKELEY AND LOS ANGELES · 1961

UNIVERSITY OF CALIFORNIA PRESS
BERKELEY AND LOS ANGELES, CALIFORNIA
CAMBRIDGE UNIVERSITY PRESS
LONDON, ENGLAND
The essays in this book have also been
published as part of *Selected Writings of
Edward Sapir in Language, Culture, and Personality*
Copyright, 1949, by
The Regents of the University of California
(First Paper-bound Edition, Fifth printing)
PRINTED IN THE UNITED STATES OF AMERICA

Editor's Introduction

This selection of Edward Sapir's best-known writings has been made at the publisher's request so that a wide circle of readers can come to know and find pleasure in his thought and style. These essays, nine in number, representative of his contributions in three fields of learning, have been chosen from the larger collection entitled *Selected Writings of Edward Sapir in Language, Culture, and Personality* published in 1949 by the University of California Press.

Sapir continues to be honored, not only by those who knew the rare quality of the man, but also by those who discover, from reading what he had to tell us, that they grow intellectually taller than they were before.

The first three essays deal with language, Sapir's principal field of study. In the long essay on language, compact and tightly written though it is, we can see something of Sapir's broad and sure grasp of the subject and of his illuminating explorations in various aspects of linguistics. The opening essay begins with a trenchant summary of the formal characteristics of language and then discusses language as an attribute of man. After taking note of various notions concerning the origin of language, Sapir goes on to an analysis of the functions of speech, and then to a description of structural and genetic classifications. The discussion of genetic affiliations among languages leads to observations on change in language and that, in turn, to the relations between language and the rest of a culture.

Practical, social considerations are central in the essay, "The Function of an International Auxiliary Language." Sapir gave much thought to this subject and his views can now be gauged in the light of events which have occurred in the years since they were first propounded. C. K. Ogden's rejoinder to Sapir appeared in the same issue of *Psyche* and also in a volume of the Psyche Miniature Series entitled *Debabelization*.

The dominant note of "The Status of Linguistics as a Science" is one which Sapir stressed in various of his writings. "Language is a cultural or social product and must be understood as such." He reminded linguists that, if their subject was to be scientifically productive and aesthetically satisfying, it could not be narrowly circumscribed, but had to be an integral and integrated part of the study of man.

"Culture, Genuine and Spurious" is an example of Sapir's comments on culture in general. In this essay he boldly offers value judgments on cultures, a procedure that was at variance with the relativistic tone of of anthropology at that period. The essay on "The Meaning of Religion" presents in noteworthy style penetrating ideas on a human characteristic.

The interplay of culture and personality was a field of study in which Sapir was a pioneer. The essay "Cultural Anthropology and Psychiatry" plots the scope and gives the rationale of culture-personality studies. The short essay on "Personality" offers definitions and suggests uses for them. The relevance of the various social sciences, especially economics, to the realities of life are discussed in "Psychiatric and Cultural Pitfalls in the Business of Getting a Living." The final essay in this collection, "The Emergence of the Concept of Personality in a Study of Cultures," offers a number of research leads which have proved to be stimulating and fruitful.

This selection of Sapir's notable essays includes only a sampling of the many that deserve the attention of a wide public. None of his technical studies in American Indian languages, and in Indo-European, Semitic, and African languages could be included within the compass of this volume. Those who want to know more about Sapir and his work may refer to *Selected Writings of Edward Sapir in Language, Culture, and Personality;* in the bibliography therein are listings of Sapir's contributions to *belles-lettres,* of his writings in musical criticism, and of his poetry. For a review of Sapir's linguistic ideas, see the article by Zellig Harris in *Language*, vol. 27 (1951), pp. 288–333.

Edward Sapir was born in Lauenberg, Germany, in 1884. When he was five years old his parents came to the United States. Sapir's early education was in Richmond, Virginia, and, after the age of ten, in the New York City schools. At the age of fourteen he entered a city-wide scholarship competition and was ranked first: "the brightest boy in New York City," said one newspaper. This scholarship award assisted him through high school and Columbia University, where he was graduated in 1904. At Columbia he came to know Franz Boas, one of the founders of American anthropology, who interested him in the anthropological approach to linguistics. With Boas' encouragement and help Sapir took an M.A. in German in 1905 and four years later received the Ph.D. in anthropology. In the summer of 1905 he made a field trip to the state of Washington to study the language of the Wishram Indians and, from that time on, much of his work concerned American Indian languages and cultures.

Following his graduate work at Columbia, Sapir spent a year as research assistant in anthropology at the University of California, Berkeley, and then two years as an instructor at the University of Pennsylvania. In 1910 he was appointed chief of the Division of Anthropology in the Geological Survey of the Canadian National Museum at Ottawa. In 1925 he was invited to the University of Chicago and six years later went to Yale University to be Sterling Professor of Anthropology and Linguistics. Before his death, February 4, 1939, Sapir had received many high academic honors, among them an honorary degree from Columbia, and the presidencies of the American Anthropological Association and of the American Linguistic Society.

The editor and publisher are grateful for Mrs. Edward Sapir's consent to the publication of the present book and also for her coöperation in supplying new biographical information. Mr. Philip Sapir has also contributed new information and has been encouraging and helpful in various ways.

Thanks are due the original publishers for permission to reprint the essays that comprise the present selection.

The Macmillan Company for "Language," from the *Encyclopaedia of the Social Sciences,* vol. 9 (1933); and for "Personality," from the *Encyclopaedia of the Social Sciences,* vol. 12 (1934).

The publishers of *Psyche* (London) for "The Function of an International Auxiliary Language," from *Psyche,* vol. 11 (1931).

Linguistic Society of America for "The Status of Linguistics as a Science," from *Language,* vol. 5 (1929).

University of Chicago Press for "Culture, Genuine and Spurious," from the *American Journal of Sociology,* vol. 29 (1924).

The American Mercury for "The Meaning of Religion," from *The American Mercury,* vol. 15 (September, 1928).

American Psychological Association for "Cultural Anthropology and Psychiatry," from the *Journal of Abnormal and Social Psychology,* vol. 27 (1932).

American Association for the Advancement of Science for "Psychiatric and Cultural Pitfalls in the Business of Getting a Living," from *Mental Health,* Publication 9, AAAS (1939).

The Journal Press for "The Emergence of a Concept of Personality in a Study of Cultures," from the *Journal of Social Psychology,* vol. 5 (1934).

Berkeley, March, 1956

D. G. M.

Editor's note.—In this second printing of the first paper-bound edition, several production errors (mainly in the Introduction) have been corrected.

The title of the present volume, selected by the publisher, should not be confused with that of *Language, Culture, and Personality, Essays in Memory of Edward Sapir.* The memorial volume, which is to be reprinted, was published in 1941 and was edited by L. Spier, A. I. Hallowell, and S. S. Newman.

Contents

LANGUAGE   1

THE FUNCTION OF AN INTERNATIONAL
AUXILIARY LANGUAGE   45

THE STATUS OF LINGUISTICS AS A SCIENCE   65

CULTURE, GENUINE AND SPURIOUS   78

THE MEANING OF RELIGION   120

CULTURAL ANTHROPOLOGY AND PSYCHIATRY   140

PERSONALITY   164

PSYCHIATRIC AND CULTURAL PITFALLS IN THE
BUSINESS OF GETTING A LIVING   172

THE EMERGENCE OF THE CONCEPT OF
PERSONALITY IN A STUDY OF CULTURES   194

Language

The gift of speech and a well-ordered language are characteristic of every known group of human beings. No tribe has ever been found which is without language, and all statements to the contrary may be dismissed as mere folklore. There seems to be no warrant whatever for the statement which is sometimes made that there are certain people whose vocabulary is so limited that they cannot get on without the supplementary use of gesture so that intelligible communication between members of such a group becomes impossible in the dark. The truth of the matter is that language is an essentially perfect means of expression and communication among every known people. Of all aspects of culture, it is a fair guess that language was the first to receive a highly developed form and that its essential perfection is a prerequisite to the development of culture as a whole.

There are such general characteristics which apply to all languages, living or extinct, written or unwritten. In the first place, language is primarily a system of phonetic symbols for the expression of communicable thought and feeling. In other words, the symbols of language are differentiated products of the vocal behavior which is associated with the larynx of

Encyclopaedia of the Social Sciences (New York, The Macmillan Company, 1933), vol. 9, pp. 155–169.

the higher mammals. As a mere matter of theory, it is conceivable that something like a linguistic structure could have been evolved out of gesture or other forms of bodily behavior. The fact that at an advanced stage in the history of the human race writing emerged in close imitation of the pattern of spoken language proved that language as a purely instrumental and logical device is not dependent on the use of articulate sound. Nevertheless, the actual history of man and a wealth of anthropological evidence indicate with overwhelming certainty that phonetic language takes precedence over all other kinds of communicative symbolism, all of which are, by comparison, either substitutive, like writing, or excessively supplementary, like the gesture accompanying speech. The speech apparatus which is used in the articulation of language is the same for all known peoples. It consists of the larynx, with its delicately adjustable glottal chords, the nose, the tongue, the hard and soft palate, the teeth, and the lips. While the original impulses leading to speech may be thought of as localized in the larynx, the finer phonetic articulations are chiefly due to the muscular activity of the tongue, an organ whose primary function has, of course, nothing whatever to do with sound production but which, in actual speech behavior, is indispensable for the development of emotionally expressive sound into what we call language. It is so indispensable, in fact, that one of the most common terms for "language" or "speech" is "tongue." Language is thus not a simple biological function even as regards the simple matter of sound production, for primary laryngeal patterns of behavior have had to be completely overhauled by the interference of lingual, labial, and nasal modifications before a "speech organ" was ready for work. Perhaps it is because this "speech organ" is a diffused and secondary network of physiological activities which do not correspond to the primary functions of the organs involved that language has been enabled to free itself from direct bodily expressiveness.

Not only are all languages phonetic in character; they are also "phonemic." Between the articulation of the voice into the phonetic sequence, which is immediately audible as a mere sensation, and the complicated patterning of phonetic sequences into such symbolically significant entities as words, phrases, and sentences there is a very interesting process of phonetic selection and generalization which is easily overlooked but which is crucial for the development of the specifically symbolic aspect of language. Language is not merely articulated sound; its significant structure is dependent upon the unconscious selection of a fixed number of "phonetic stations" or sound units These are in actual behavior individually modifiable; but the essential point is that through the unconscious selection of sounds as phonemes, definite psychological barriers are erected between various phonetic stations, so that speech ceases to be an expressive flow of sound and becomes a symbolic composition with limited materials or units. The analogy with musical theory seems quite fair. Even the most resplendent and dynamic symphony is built up of tangibly distinct musical entities or notes which, in the physical world, flow into each other in an indefinite continuum but which, in the world of aesthetic composition and appreciation, are definitely bounded off against each other, so that they may enter into an intricate mathematics of significant relationships. The phonemes of a language are, in principle, distinct systems peculiar to the given language, and its words must be made up, in unconscious theory if not always in actualized behavior, of these phonemes. Languages differ very widely in their phonemic structure. But whatever the details of these structures may be, the important fact remains that there is no known language which has not a perfectly definite phonemic system. The difference between a sound and a phoneme can be illustrated by a simple example in English. If the word "matter" is pronounced in a slovenly fashion as in the phrase "What's the matter?" the *t* sound, not being pronounced with the proper amount of energy required to bring out its physical characteristics, tends to slip into a *d*. Nevertheless, this phonetic *d* will not be felt as a functional *d* but as a variety of *t* of a particular type of expressiveness. Obviously the functional relation between the proper *t* sound of such a word as "matter" and its *d* variant is quite other than the relation of the *t* of such a word as "town" and the *d* of "down." In every known language it is possible to distinguish merely phonetic variations, whether expressive or not, from symbolically functional ones of a phonemic order.

In all known languages, phonemes are built up into distinct and arbitrary sequences which are at once recognized by speakers as meaningful symbols of reference. In English, for instance, the sequence *g* plus *o* in the word "go" is an unanalyzable unit and the meaning attaching to the symbol cannot be derived by relating to each other values which might be imputed to the *g* and to the *o* independently. In other words, while the mechanical functional units of language are phonemes, the true units of language as symbolism are conventional groupings of such phonemes. The size of these units and the laws of their mechanical structure vary widely in their different languages and their limiting conditions may be said to constitute the phonemic mechanics, or "phonology," of a particular language. But the fundamental theory of sound symbolism remains the same everywhere. The formal behavior of the irreducible symbol also varies within wide limits in the languages of the world. Such a unit may be either a complete word, as in the English example already given, or a significant element like the suffix *ness* of "goodness." Between the meaningful and unanalyzable word or word element and the integrated meaning of continuous discourse lies the whole complicated field of the formal procedures which are intuitively employed by the speakers of a language in order to build up aesthetically and functionally satisfying symbol sequences out of the theoretically isolable units These procedures constitute grammar, which may be defined as the sum total of formal economies intuitively recognized by the speakers of a language. There seem to be no types of cultural patterns which vary more surprisingly and with a greater exuberance of detail than the morphologies of the known languages. In spite of endless differences of detail, however, it may justly be said that all grammars have the same degree of fixity. One language may be more complex or difficult grammatically than another, but there is no meaning whatever in the statement which is sometimes made that one language is more grammatical, or form bound, than another. Our rationalizations of the structure of our own language lead to a self-consciousness of speech and of academic discipline which are of course interesting psychological and social phenomena in themselves but have very little to do with the question of form in language.

Besides these general formal characteristics language has certain psychological qualities which make it peculiarly important for the student of social science In the first place, language is felt to be a perfect symbolic system, in a perfectly homogeneous medium, for the handling of all references and meanings that a given culture is capable of, whether these be in the form of actual communications or in that of such ideal substitutes of communication as thinking. The content of every culture is expressible in its language and there are no linguistic materials whether as to content or form which are not felt to symbolize actual meanings, whatever may be the attitude of those who belong to other cultures. New cultural experiences frequently make it necessary to enlarge the resources of a language, but such enlargement is never an arbitrary addition to the materials and forms already present; it is merely a further application of principles already in use and in many cases little more than a metaphorical extension of old terms and meanings. It is highly important to realize that once the form of a language is established it can discover meanings for its speakers which are not simply traceable to the given quality of experience itself but must be explained to a large extent as the projection of potential meanings into the raw material of experience. If a man who has never seen more than a single elephant in the course of his life, nevertheless speaks without the slightest hesitation of ten elephants or a million elephants or a herd of elephants or of elephants walking two by two or three by three or of generations of elephants, it is obvious that language has the power to analyze experience into theoretically dissociable elements and to create that world of the potential intergrading with the actual which enables human beings to transcend the immediately given in their individual experiences and to join in a larger common understanding. This common understanding constitutes culture, which cannot be adequately defined by a description of those more colorful patterns of behavior in society which lie open to observation. Language is heuristic, not merely in the simple sense which this example suggests, but in the much more far-reaching sense that its forms predetermine for us certain modes of observation and interpretation. This means of course that as our scientific experience grows we must learn to fight the implications of language. "The grass waves in the wind" is shown by its linguistic form to be a member of the same relational class of experiences as "The man works in the house." As an interim solution of the problem of expressing the experience referred to in this sentence it is clear that the language has proved useful, for it has made significant use of certain symbols of conceptual relation, such as agency and location. If we feel the sentence to be poetic or metaphorical, it is largely because other more complex types of experience with their appropriate symbolisms of reference enable us to reinterpret the situation and to say, for instance, "The grass is waved by the wind" or "The wind causes the grass to wave." The point is that no matter how sophisticated our modes of interpretation become, we never really get beyond the projection and continuous transfer of relations suggested by the forms of our speech. After all, to say "Friction causes such and such a result" is not very different from saying "The grass waves in the wind." Language is at one and the same time helping and retarding us in our exploration of experience, and the details of these processes of help and hindrance are deposited in the subtler meanings of different cultures.

A further psychological characteristic of language is the fact that while it may be looked upon as a symbolic system which reports or refers to or otherwise substitutes for direct experience, it does not as a matter of actual behavior stand apart from or run parallel to direct experience but completely interpenetrates with it. This is indicated by the widespread feeling, particularly among primitive people, of that virtual identity or close correspondence of word and thing which leads to the magic of spells. On our own level it is generally difficult to make a complete divorce between objective reality and our linguistic symbols of reference to it; and things, qualities, and events are on the whole felt to be what they are called. For the normal person every experience, real or potential, is saturated with verbalism. This explains why so many lovers of nature, for instance, do not feel that they are truly in touch with it until they have mastered the names of a great many flowers and trees, as though the primary world of reality were a verbal one and as though one could not get close to nature unless one first mastered the terminology which somehow magically expresses it. It is this constant interplay between language and experience which removes language from the cold status of such purely and simply symbolic systems as mathematical symbolism or flag signaling. This interpenetration is not only an intimate associative fact; it is also a contextual one. It is important to realize that language may not only refer to experience or even mold, interpret, and discover experience, but that it also substitutes for it in the sense that in those sequences of interpersonal behavior which form the greater part of our daily lives speech and action supplement each other and do each other's work in a web of unbroken pattern. If one says to me "Lend me a dollar," I may hand over the money without a word or I may give it with an accompanying "Here it is" or I may say "I haven't got it" or "I'll give it to you tomorrow." Each of these responses is structurally equivalent, if one thinks of the larger behavior pattern. It is clear that if language is in its analyzed form

a symbolic system of reference, it is far from being
merely that if we consider the psychological part
that it plays in continuous behavior. The reason
for this almost unique position of intimacy which
language holds among all known symbolisms is probably the fact that it is learned in the earliest years of
childhood.

It is because it is learned early and piecemeal, in
constant association with the color and the requirements of actual contexts, that language, in spite of
its quasi-mathematical form, is rarely a purely referential organization. It tends to be so only in scientific discourse, and even there it may be seriously
doubted whether the ideal of pure reference is ever
attained by language. Ordinary speech is directly expressive and the purely formal pattern of sounds,
words, grammatical forms, phrases and sentences
are always to be thought of as compounded by in-
tended or unintended symbolisms of expression, if
they are to be understood fully from the standpoint
of behavior. The choice of words in a particular context may convey the opposite of what they mean on
the surface. The same external message is differently
interpreted according to whether the speaker has
this or that psychological status in his personal relations, or whether such primary expressions as those of
affection or anger or fear may inform the spoken
words with a significance which completely transcends their normal value. On the whole, however,
there is no danger that the expressive character of
language will be overlooked. It is too obvious a fact
to call for much emphasis. What is often overlooked

and is, as a matter of fact, not altogether easy to understand is that the quasi-mathematical patterns, as we have called them, of the grammarian's language, unreal as these are in a contextual sense, have, nevertheless, a tremendous intuitive vitality; and that these patterns, never divorced in experience from the expressive ones, are nevertheless easily separated from them by the normal individual. The fact that almost any word or phrase can be made to take on an infinite variety of meanings seems to indicate that in all language behavior there are intertwined, in enormously complex patterns, isolable patterns of two distinct orders These may be roughly defined as patterns of reference and patterns of expression.

That language is a perfect symbolism of experience, that in the actual context of behavior it cannot be divorced from action and that it is the carrier of an infinitely nuanced expressiveness are universally valid psychological facts There is a fourth general psychological peculiarity which applies more particularly to the languages of sophisticated peoples. This is the fact that the referential form systems which are actualized in language behavior do not need speech in its literal sense in order to preserve their substantial integrity. The history of writing is in essence the long attempt to develop an independent symbolism on the basis of graphic representation, followed by the slow and begrudging realization that spoken language is a more powerful symbolism than any graphic one can possibly be and that true progress in the art of writing lay in the virtual abandonment of the principle with which it originally started.

Effective systems of writing, whether alphabetic or not, are more or less exact transfers of speech. The original language system may maintain itself in other and remoter transfers, one of the best examples of these being the Morse telegraph code. It is a very interesting fact that the principle of linguistic transfer is not entirely absent even among the unlettered peoples of the world. Some at least of the drum signal and horn signal systems of the West African natives are in principle transfers of the organizations of speech, often in minute phonetic detail.

Many attempts have been made to unravel the origin of language, but most of these are hardly more than exercises of the speculative imagination. Linguists as a whole have lost interest in the problem, and this for two reasons. In the first place, it has come to be realized that we have no truly primitive languages in a psychological sense, that modern researches in archaeology have indefinitely extended the time of man's cultural past and that it is therefore vain to go much beyond the perspective opened up by the study of actual languages. In the second place, our knowledge of psychology, particularly of the symbolic processes in general, is not felt to be sound enough or far-reaching enough to help materially with the problem of the emergence of speech. It is probable that the origin of language is not a problem that can be solved out of the resources of linguistics alone but that it is essentially a particular case of a much wider problem of the genesis of symbolic behavior and of the specialization of such behavior in the laryngeal region, which may be presumed to have had only expressive functions to begin with. Perhaps a close study of the behavior of very young children under controlled conditions may provide some valuable hints, but it seems dangerous to reason from such experiments to the behavior of precultural man. It is more likely that the kinds of studies which are now in progress of the behavior of the higher apes will help to give us some idea of the genesis of speech.

The most popular earlier theories were the interjectional and onomatopoetic theories. The former derived speech from involuntary cries of an expressive nature, while the latter maintained that the words of actual language are conventionalized forms of imitation of the sounds of nature. Both of these theories suffer from two fatal defects. While it is true that both interjectional and onomatopoetic elements are found in most languages, they are always relatively unimportant and tend to contrast somewhat with the more normal materials of language. The very fact that they are constantly being formed anew seems to indicate that they belong rather to the directly expressive layer of speech which intercrosses with the main level of referential symbolism. The second difficulty is even more serious. The essential problem of the origin of speech is not to attempt to discover the kinds of vocal elements which constitute the historical nucleus of language. It is rather to point out how vocal articulations of any sort could become dissociated from their original expressive value. About all that can be said at present is that while speech as a finished organization is a distinctly human achievement, its roots probably lie in the power of the higher apes to solve specific problems by abstracting general forms or schemata from the details of given situations; that the habit of interpreting certain selected elements in a situation as signs of a desired total one gradually led in early man to a dim feeling for symbolism; and that, in the long run and for reasons which can hardly be guessed at, the elements of experience which were most often interpreted in a symbolic sense came to be the largely useless or supplementary vocal behavior that must have often attended significant action. According to this point of view language is not so much directly developed out of vocal expression as it is an actualization in terms of vocal expression of the tendency to master reality, not by direct and *ad hoc* handling of this element but by the reduction of experience to familiar form. Vocal expression is only superficially the same as language. The tendency to derive speech from emotional expression has not led to anything tangible in the way of scientific theory and the attempt must now be made to see in language the slowly evolved product of a peculiar technique or tendency which may be called the symbolic one, and to see the relatively meaningless or incomplete part as a sign of the whole. Language, then, is what it is essentially, not because of its admirable expressive power but in spite of it. Speech as behavior is a wonderfully complex blend of two pattern systems, the symbolic and the expressive, neither of which could have developed to its present perfection without the interference of the other.

It is difficult to see adequately the functions of language, because it is so deeply rooted in the whole of human behavior that it may be suspected that there is little in the functional side of our conscious behavior in which language does not play its part. The primary function of language is generally said to be communication. There can be no quarrel with this so long as it is distinctly understood that there may be effective communication without overt speech and that language is highly relevant to situations which are not obviously of a communicative sort. To say that thought, which is hardly possible in any sustained sense without the symbolic organization brought by language, is that form of communication in which the speaker and the person addressed are identified in one person is not far from begging the question. The autistic speech of children seems to show that the purely communicative aspect of language has been exaggerated. It is best to admit that language is primarily a vocal actualization of the tendency to see realities symbolically, that it is precisely this quality which renders it a fit instrument for communication and that it is in the actual give and take of social intercourse that it has been complicated and refined into the form in which it is known today. Besides the very general function which language fulfills in the spheres of thought, communication, and expression which are implicit in its very nature, there may be pointed out a number of special derivatives of these which are of particular interest to students of society.

Language is a great force of socialization, probably

the greatest that exists. By this is meant not merely the obvious fact that significant social intercourse is hardly possible without language but that the mere fact of a common speech serves as a peculiarly potent symbol of the social solidarity of those who speak the language. The psychological significance of this goes far beyond the association of particular languages with nationalities, political entities, or smaller local groups. In between the recognized dialect or language as a whole and the individualized speech of a given individual lies a kind of linguistic unit which is not often discussed by the linguist but which is of the greatest importance to social psychology. This is the subform of a language which is current among a group of people who are held together by ties of common interest. Such a group may be a family, the undergraduates of a college, a labor union, the underworld in a large city, the members of a club, a group of four or five friends who hold together through life in spite of differences of professional interest, and untold thousands of other kinds of groups. Each of these tends to develop peculiarities of speech which have the symbolic function of somehow distinguishing the group from the larger group into which its members might be too completely absorbed. The complete absence of linguistic indices of such small groups is obscurely felt as a defect or sign of emotional poverty. Within the confines of a particular family, for instance, the name "Georgy," having once been mispronounced "Doody" in childhood, may take on the latter form forever after; and this unofficial pronunciation of a familiar name as applied to a particular person becomes a very important symbol indeed of the solidarity of a particular family and of the continuance of the sentiment that keeps its members together. A stranger cannot lightly take on the privilege of saying "Doody" if the members of the family feel that he is not entitled to go beyond the degree of familiarity symbolized by the use of "Georgy" or "George." Again, no one is entitled to say "trig" or "math" who has not gone through such familiar and painful experiences as a high school or undergraduate student. The use of such words at once declares the speaker a member of an unorganized but psychologically real group. A self-made mathematician has hardly the right to use the word "math" in referring to his own interests because the student overtones of the word do not properly apply to him. The extraordinary importance of minute linguistic differences for the symbolization of psychologically real as contrasted with politically or sociologically official groups is intuitively felt by most people. "He talks like us" is equivalent to saying "He is one of us."

There is another important sense in which language is a socializer beyond its literal use as a means of communication. This is in the establishment of rapport between the members of a physical group, such as a house party. It is not what is said that matters so much as that something is said. Particularly where cultural understandings of an intimate sort are somewhat lacking among the members of a physical group it is felt to be important that the lack be made good by a constant supply of small talk. This caressing or reassuring quality of speech in general, even where no one has anything of moment to communicate, reminds us how much more language is than a mere technique of communication. Nothing better shows how completely the life of man as an animal made over by culture is dominated by the verbal substitutes for the physical world.

The use of language in cultural accumulation and historical transmission is obvious and important. This applies not only to sophisticated levels but to primitive ones as well. A great deal of the cultural stock in trade of a primitive society is presented in a more or less well defined linguistic form. Proverbs, medicine formulae, standardized prayers, folk tales, standardized speeches, song texts, genealogies are some of the more overt forms which language takes as a culture-preserving instrument. The pragmatic ideal of education, which aims to reduce the influence of standardized lore to a minimum and to get the individual to educate himself through as direct a contact as possible with the realities of his environment, is certainly not realized among the primitives, who are often as word-bound as the humanistic tradition itself. Few cultures perhaps have gone to the length of the classical Chinese culture or of the rabbinical Jewish culture in making the word do duty for the thing or the personal experience as the ultimate unit of reality. Modern civilization as a whole, with its schools, its libraries, and its endless stores of knowledge, opinion, and sentiment stored up in verbalized form, would be unthinkable without language made eternal as document. On the whole, we probably tend to exaggerate the differences between "high" and "low" cultures or saturated and emergent cultures in the matter of traditionally conserved verbal authority. The enormous differences that seem to exist are rather differences in the outward form and content of the cultures themselves than in the psychological relation which obtains between the individual and his culture.

In spite of the fact that language acts as a socializing and uniformizing force, it is at the same time the most potent single known factor for the growth of individuality. The fundamental quality of one's voice, the phonetic patterns of speech, the speed and relative smoothness of articulation, the length and build of the sentences, the character and range of the vocabulary, the scholastic consistency of the words used, the readiness with which words respond to the requirements of the social environment, in particular the suitability of one's language to the language habits of the persons addressed—all these are so many complex indicators of the personality. "Actions speak louder than words" may be an excellent maxim from the pragmatic point of view but betrays little insight into the nature of speech. The language habits of people are by no means irrelevant as unconscious indicators of the more important traits of their personalities, and the folk is psychologically wiser than the adage in paying a great deal of attention, willingly or not, to the psychological significance of a man's language. The normal person is never convinced by the mere content of speech but is very sensitive to many of the implications of language behavior, however feebly (if at all) these may have been consciously analyzed. All in all, it is not too much to say that one of the really important functions of language is to be constantly declaring to society the psychological place held by all of its members.

Besides this more general type of personality expression or fulfillment there is to be kept in mind the important role which language plays as a substitutive means of expression for those individuals who have a greater than normal difficulty in adjusting to the environment in terms of primary action patterns. Even in the most primitive cultures the strategic word is likely to be more powerful than the direct blow. It is unwise to speak too blithely of "mere" words, for to do so may be to imperil the value and perhaps the very existence of civilization and personality.

The languages of the world may be classified either structurally or genetically. An adequate structural analysis is an intricate matter and no classification seems to have been suggested which does justice to the bewildering variety of known forms. It is useful to recognize three distinct criteria of classification: the relative degree of synthesis or elaboration of the words of the language; the degree to which the various parts of a word are welded together; and the extent to which the fundamental relational concepts of the language are directly expressed as such. As regards synthesis, languages range all the way from the isolating type, in which the single word is essentially unanalyzable, to the type represented by many American Indian languages in which the single word is functionally often the equivalent of a sentence with many concrete references that would, in most languages, require the use of a number of words. Four stages of synthesis may be conveniently recognized: the isolating type, the weakly synthetic type, the fully synthetic type, and the polysynthetic type. The classical example of the first type is Chinese, which does not allow the words of the language to be modified by internal changes or the addition of prefixed or suffixed elements to express such concepts as those of number, tense, mode, case relation, and the like. This seems to be one of the more uncommon types of language and is best represented by a number of languages in eastern Asia. Besides Chinese itself, Siamese, Burmese, modern Tibetan, Annamite, and Khmer, or Cambodian, may be given as examples. The older view, which regarded such languages as representing a peculiarly primitive stage in the evolution of language, may now be dismissed as antiquated. All evidence points to the contrary hypothesis that such languages are the logically extreme analytic developments of more synthetic languages which because of processes of phonetic disintegration have had to reëxpress by analytical means combinations of ideas originally expressed within the framework of the single word. The weakly synthetic type of language is best represented by the most familiar modern languages of Europe, such as English, French, Spanish, Italian, German, Dutch, and Danish. Such languages modify words to some extent but have only a moderate formal elaboration of the word. The plural formations of English and French, for instance, are relatively simple and the tense and modal systems of all the languages of this type tend to use analytic methods as supplementary to the older synthetic one. The third group of languages is represented by such languages as Arabic and the earlier Indo-European languages, like Sanskrit, Latin, and Greek. These are all languages of great formal complexity, in which classificatory ideas, such as sex gender, number, case relations, tense, and mood, are expressed with considerable nicety and in a great variety of ways. Because of the rich formal implications of the single word the sentence tends not to be so highly energized and ordered as in the first mentioned types. Lastly, the polysynthetic languages add to the formal complexity of the treatment of fundamental relational ideas the power to arrange a number of logically distinct, concrete ideas into an ordered whole within the confines of a single word. Eskimo and Algonquin are classical examples of this type.

From the standpoint of the mechanical cohesiveness with which the elements of words are united languages may be conveniently grouped into four types. The first of these, in which there is no such process of combination, is the isolating type already referred to. To the second group of languages belong all those in which the word can be adequately analyzed into a mechanical sum of elements, each of which has its more or less clearly established meaning and each of which is regularly used in all other words into which the associated notion enters. These are the so-called agglutinative languages. The majority of languages seem to use the agglutinative technique, which has the great advantage of combining logical analysis with economy of means. The Altaic languages, of which Turkish is a good example, and the Bantu languages of Africa are agglutinative in form.

In the third type, the so-called inflective languages, the degree of union between the radical element or stem of the word and the modifying prefixes or suffixes is greater than in the agglutinative languages, so that it becomes difficult in many cases to isolate the stem and set it off against the accreted elements. More important than this, however, is the fact that there is more or less of a one-to-one correspondence between the linguistic element and the notion referred to than in the agglutinative languages. In Latin, for instance, the notion of plurality is expressed in a great variety of ways which seem to have little phonetic connection with each other. For example, the final vowel or diphthong of *equi* (horses), *dona* (gifts), *mensae* (tables), and the final vowel and consonant of *hostes* (enemies) are functionally equivalent elements the distribution of which is dependent on purely formal and historical factors which have no logical relevance. Furthermore in the verb the notion of plurality is quite differently expressed, as in the last two consonants of *amant* (they love). It used to be fashionable to contrast in a favorable sense the "chemical" qualities of such inflective languages as Latin and Greek with the soberly mechanical quality of such languages as Turkish. But these evaluations may now be dismissed as antiquated and subjective. They were obviously due to the fact that scholars who wrote in English, French, and German were not above rationalizing the linguistic structures with which they were most familiar into a position of ideal advantage.

As an offshoot of the inflective languages may be considered a fourth group, those in which the processes of welding, due to the operation of complex phonetic laws, have gone so far as to result in the creation of patterns of internal change of the nuclear elements of speech. Such familiar English examples as the words "sing," "sang," "sung," "song" will serve to give some idea of the nature of these structures, which may be termed "symbolistic." The kinds of internal change which may be recognized are changes in vocalic quality, changes in consonants, changes in quantity, various types of reduplication or repetition, changes in stress accent, and, as in Chinese and many African languages, changes in pitch. The classical example of this type of language is Arabic, in which, as in the other Semitic languages, nuclear meanings are expressed by sequences or consonants, which have, however, to be connected by significant vowels whose sequence patterns establish fixed functions independent of the meanings conveyed by the consonantal framework.

Elaboration and technique of word analysis are perhaps of less logical and psychological significance than the selection and treatment of fundamental relational concepts for grammatical treatment. It would be very difficult, however, to devise a satisfactory conceptual classification of languages because of the extraordinary diversity of the concepts and classifications of ideas which are illustrated in linguistic form. In the Indo-European and Semitic languages, for instance, noun classification on the basis of gender is a vital principle of structure; but in most of the other languages of the world this principle is absent, although other methods of noun classification are found. Again, tense or case relations may be formally important in one language, for example, Latin, but of relatively little grammatical importance in another, although the logical references implied by such forms must naturally somehow be taken care of in the economy of the language as, for instance, by the use of specific words within the framework of the sentence. Perhaps the most fundamental conceptual basis of classification is that of the expression of fundamental syntactic relations as such versus their expression in necessary combination with notions of a concrete order. In Latin, for example, the notion of the subject of a predicate is never purely expressed in a formal sense, because there is no distinctive symbol for this relation. It is impossible to render it without at the same time defining the number and gender of the subject of the sentence. There are languages, however, in which syntactic relations are expressed purely, without admixture of implications of a nonrelational sort. We may speak therefore of pure relational languages as contrasted with mixed relational languages. Most of the languages with which we are familiar belong to the latter category. It goes without saying that such a conceptual classification has no direct relation to the other two types of classification which we have mentioned.

The genetic classification of languages is one which attempts to arrange the languages of the world in groups and subgroups in accordance with the main lines of historical connection, which can be worked out either on the basis of documentary evidence or of a careful comparison of the languages studied. Because of the far-reaching effect of slow phonetic changes and of other causes languages which were originally nothing but dialects of the same form of speech have diverged so widely that it is not apparent that they are but specialized developments of a single prototype. An enormous amount of work has been done in the genetic classification and subclassification of the languages of the world, but very many problems still await research and solution. At the present time it is known definitely that there are certain very large linguistic groups, or families, as they are often called, the members of which may, roughly speaking, be looked upon as lineally descended from languages which can be theoretically reconstructed in their main phonetic and structural outlines. It is obvious, however, that languages may so diverge as to leave little trace of their original relationship. It is therefore very dangerous to assume that languages are not, at last analysis, divergent members of a single genetic group merely because the evidence is negative. The only contrast that is legitimate is between languages known to be historically related and languages not known to be so related. Languages known to be related cannot be legitimately contrasted with languages known not to be related.

Because of the fact that languages have differentiated at different rates and because of the important effects of cultural diffusion, which have brought it about that strategically placed languages, such as Arabic, Latin, and English, have spread over large parts of the earth at the expense of others, very varied conditions are found to prevail in regard to the distribution of linguistic families. In Europe, for instance, there are only two linguistic families of importance represented today, the Indo-European languages and the Ugro-Finnic languages, of which Finnish and Hungarian are examples. The Basque dialects of southern France and northern Spain are the survivors of another and apparently isolated group. On the other hand, in aboriginal America the linguistic differentiation is extreme and a surprisingly large number of essentially unrelated linguistic families must be recognized. Some of the families occupy very small areas, while others, such as the Algonquin and the Athabaskan languages of North America, are spread over a large territory. The technique of establishing linguistic families and of working out the precise relationship of the languages included in these families is too difficult to be gone into here. It suffices to say that random word comparisons are of little importance. Experience shows that very precise phonetic relations can be worked out between the languages of a group and that, on the whole, fundamental morphological features tend to preserve themselves over exceedingly long periods of time. Thus modern Lithuanian is in structure, vocabulary and, to a large extent, even phonemic pattern very much the kind of a language which must be assumed as the prototype for the Indo-European languages as a whole.

In spite of the fact that structural classifications are, in theory, unrelated to genetic ones and in spite of the fact that languages can be shown to have influenced each other, not only in phonetics and vocabulary but also to an appreciable extent in structure, it is not often found that the languages of a genetic group exhibit utterly irreconcilable structures. Thus even English, which is one of the least conservative of Indo-European languages, has many far-reaching points of structure in common with as remote a language as Sanskrit in contrast, say, to Basque or Finnish. Again, different as are Assyrian, modern Arabic, and the Semitic languages of Abyssinia, they exhibit numerous points of resemblance in phonetics, vocabulary, and structure which set them off at once from, say, Turkish or the Negro languages of the Nile headwaters.

The complete rationale of linguistic change, involving as it does many of the most complex processes of psychology and sociology, has not yet been satisfactorily worked out, but there are a number of general processes that emerge with sufficient clarity. For practical purposes, inherent changes may be distinguished from changes due to contact with other linguistic communities. There can be no hard line of division between these two groups of changes because every individual's language is a distinct psychological entity in itself, so that all inherent changes are likely, at last analysis, to be peculiarly remote or subtle forms of change due to contact. The distinction, however, has great practical value, all the more so as there is a tendency among anthropologists and sociologists to operate far too hastily with wholesale linguistic changes due to external ethnic and cultural influences. The enormous amount of study that has been lavished on the history of particular languages and groups of languages shows very clearly that the most powerful differentiating factors are not outside influences, as ordinarily understood, but rather the very slow but powerful unconscious changes in certain directions which seem to be implicit in the phonemic systems and morphologies of the languages themselves. These "drifts" are powerfully conditioned by unconscious formal feelings and are made necessary by the inability of human beings to actualize ideal patterns in a permanently set fashion.

Linguistic changes may be analyzed into phonetic changes, changes in form, and changes in vocabulary. Of these the phonetic changes seem to be the most important and the most removed from direct observation. The factors which lead to these phonetic changes are probably exceedingly complex and no doubt include the operation of obscure symbolisms which define the relation of various age groups to each other. Not all phonetic changes, however, can be explained in terms of social symbolism. It seems that many of them are due to the operation of unconscious economies in actualizing sounds or combinations of sounds. The most impressive thing about internal phonetic change is its high degree of regularity. It is this regularity, whatever its ultimate cause, that is more responsible than any other single factor for the enviable degree of exactness which linguistics has attained as a historical discipline. Changes in grammatical form often follow in the wake of destructive phonetic changes. In many cases it can be seen how irregularities produced by the disintegrating effect of phonetic change are ironed out by the analogical spread of more regular forms. The cumulative effect of these corrective changes is quite sensibly to modify the structure of the language in many details and sometimes even in its fundamental features. Changes in vocabulary are due to a great variety of causes, most of which are of a cultural rather than of a strictly linguistic nature. The too frequent use of a word, for instance, may reduce it to a commonplace term, so that it needs to be replaced by a new word. On the other hand, changes of attitude may make certain words with their traditional overtones of meaning unacceptable to the younger generation, so that they tend to become obsolete. Probably the most important single source of changes in vocabulary is the creation of new words on analogies which have spread from a few specific words.

Of the linguistic changes due to the more obvious types of contact the one which seems to have played the most important part in the history of language is the "borrowing" of words across linguistic frontiers. This borrowing naturally goes hand in hand with cultural diffusion. An analysis of the provenience of the words of a given language is frequently an important index of the direction of cultural influence. Our English vocabulary, for instance, is very richly stratified in a cultural sense. The various layers of early Latin, mediaeval French, humanistic Latin and Greek, and modern French borrowings constitute a fairly accurate gauge of the time, extent, and nature of the various foreign cultural influences which have helped to mold the English civilization. The notable lack of German loan words in English until a very recent period, as contrasted with the large number of Italian words which were adopted at the time of the Renaissance and later, is again a historically significant fact. By the diffusion of culturally important words, such as those referring to art, literature, the church, military affairs, sport, and business, important transnational vocabularies have grown up which do something to combat the isolating effect of the large number of languages which are still spoken in the modern world. Such borrowings have taken place in all directions, but the number of truly important source languages is surprisingly small. Among the more important of them are Chinese, which has saturated the vocabularies of Korean, Japanese, and Annamite; Sanskrit, whose influence on the cultural vocabulary of central Asia, India, and Indo-China, has been enormous; Arabic, Greek, Latin, and French. English, Spanish, and Italian have also been of great importance as agencies of cultural transmission, but their influence seems less far-reaching than that of the languages mentioned above. The cultural influence of a language is not always in direct proportion to its intrinsic literary interest or to the cultural place which its speakers have held in the history of the world. For example, while Hebrew is the carrier of a peculiarly significant culture, actually it has not had as important an influence on other languages of Asia as Aramaic, a sister language of the Semitic stock.

The phonetic influence exerted by a foreign language may be very considerable, and there is a great deal of evidence to show that dialectic peculiarities have often originated as a result of the unconscious transfer of phonetic habits from the language in which one was brought up to that which has been adopted later in life. Apart, however, from such complete changes in speech is the remarkable fact that distinctive phonetic features tend to be distributed over wide areas regardless of the vocabularies and structures of the languages involved. One of the most striking examples of this type of distribution is found among the Indian languages of the Pacific coast of California, Oregon, Washington, British Columbia, and southern Alaska. Here are a large number of absolutely distinct languages belonging to a number of genetically unrelated stocks, so far as we are able to tell, which nevertheless have many important and distinctive phonetic features in common. An analogous fact is the distribution of certain peculiar phonetic features in both the Slavic languages and the Ugro-Finnic languages, which are unrelated to them. Such processes of phonetic diffusion must be due to the influence exerted by bilingual speakers, who act as unconscious agents for the spread of phonetic habits over wide areas. Primitive man is not isolated, and bilingualism is probably as important a factor in the contact of primitive groups as it is on more sophisticated levels.

Opinions differ as to the importance of the purely morphological influence exerted by one language on another in contrast with the more external type of phonetic and lexical influence. Undoubtedly such influences must be taken into account, but so far they have not been shown to operate on any great scale. In spite of the centuries of contact, for instance, between Semitic and Indo-European languages we know of no language which is definitely a blend of the structures of these two stocks. Similarly, while Japanese is flooded with Chinese loan words, there seems to be no structural influence of Chinese on Japanese.

A type of influence which is neither exactly one of vocabulary nor of linguistic form, in the ordinary sense of the word, and to which insufficient attention has so far been called, is that of meaning pattern. It is a remarkable fact of modern European culture, for instance, that while the actual terms used for certain ideas may vary enormously from language to language, the range of significance of these equivalent terms tends to be very similar, so that to a large extent the vocabulary of one language tends to be a psychological and cultural translation of the vocabulary of another. A simple example of this sort would be the translation of such terms as "Your Excellency" to equivalent but etymologically unrelated terms in Russian. Another instance of this kind would be the interesting parallelism in nomenclature between the kinship terms of affinity in English, French, and German. Such terms as "mother-in-law," "belle-mère," and "Schwiegermutter" are not, strictly speaking, equivalent either as to etymology or literal meaning but they are patterned in exactly the same manner. Thus "mother-in-law" and "father-in-law" are parallel in nomenclature to "belle-mère" and "beau-père" and to "Schwiegermutter" and "Schwiegervater." These terms clearly illustrate the diffusion of a lexical pattern which in turn probably expresses a growing feeling of the sentimental equivalent of blood relatives and relatives by marriage.

The importance of language as a whole for the definition, expression, and transmission of culture is undoubted. The relevance of linguistic details, in both content and form, for the profounder understanding of culture is also clear. It does not follow, however, that there is a simple correspondence between the form of a language and the form of the culture of those who speak it. The tendency to see linguistic categories as directly expressive of overt cultural outlines, which seems to have come into fashion among certain sociologists and anthropologists, should be resisted as in no way warranted by the actual facts. There is no general correlation between cultural type and linguistic structure. So far as can be seen, isolating or agglutinative or inflective types of speech are possible on any level of civilization. Nor does the presence or absence of grammatical gender for example, seem to have any relevance for our understanding of the social organization or religion or folklore of the associated peoples. If there were any such parallelism as has sometimes been maintained, it would be quite impossible to understand the rapidity with which culture diffuses in spite of profound linguistic differences between the borrowing and giving communities.

The cultural significance of linguistic form, in other words, lies on a much more submerged level than on the overt one of definite cultural pattern. It is only very rarely, as a matter of fact, that it can be pointed out how a cultural trait has had some influence on the fundamental structure of a language. To a certain extent this lack of correspondence may be due to the fact that linguistic changes do not proceed at the same rate as most cultural changes, which are on the whole far more rapid. Short of yielding to another language which takes its place, linguistic organization, largely because it is unconscious, tends to maintain itself indefinitely and does not allow its fundamental formal categories to be seriously influenced by changing cultural needs. If the forms of culture and language were, then, in complete correspondence with each other, the nature of the processes making for linguistic and cultural changes respectively would soon bring about a lack of necessary correspondence. This is exactly what is found as a mere matter of descriptive fact. Logically it is indefensible that the masculine, feminine, and neuter genders of German and Russian should be allowed to continue their sway in the modern world; but any intellectualist attempt to weed out these unnecessary genders would obviously be fruitless, for the normal speaker does not actually feel the clash which the logician requires.

It is another matter when we pass from general form to the detailed content of a language. Vocabulary is a very sensitive index of the culture of a people and changes of the meaning, loss of old words, the creation and borrowing of new ones are all dependent on the history of culture itself. Languages differ widely in the nature of their vocabularies. Distinctions which seem inevitable to us may be utterly ignored in languages which reflect an entirely different type of culture, while these in turn insist on distinctions which are all but unintelligible to us.

Such differences of vocabulary go far beyond the names of cultural objects such as arrow point, coat of armor, or gunboat. They apply just as well to the mental world. It would be difficult in some languages, for instance, to express the distinction which we feel between "to kill" and "to murder," for the simple reason that the underlying legal philosophy which determines our use of these words does not seem natural to all societies. Abstract terms, which are so necessary to our thinking, may be infrequent in a language whose speakers formulate their behavior on more pragmatic lines. On the other hand, the question of presence or absence of abstract nouns may be bound up with the fundamental form of the language; and there exist a large number of primitive languages whose structure allows of the very ready creation and use of abstract nouns of quality or action.

There are many language patterns of a special sort which are of interest to the social scientist. One of these is the tendency to create tabus for certain words or names. A very widespread custom, for instance, among primitive peoples is the tabu which is placed not only on the use of the name of a person recently deceased but of any word that is etymologically connected in the feeling of the speakers with such a name. This means that ideas have often to be expressed by circumlocutions, or that terms must be borrowed from neighboring dialects. Sometimes certain names or words are too holy to be pronounced except under very special conditions, and curious patterns of behavior develop which are designed to prevent one from making use of such interdicted terms. An example of this is the Jewish custom of pronouncing the Hebrew name for God, not as Yahwe or Jehovah but as Adonai, "My Lord." Such customs seem strange to us but equally strange to many primitive communities would be our extraordinary reluctance to pronounce obscene words under normal social conditions.

Another class of special linguistic phenomena is the use of esoteric language devices, such as passwords or technical terminologies for ceremonial attitudes or practices. Among the Eskimo, for instance, the medicine man has a peculiar vocabulary which is not understood by those who are not members of his guild. Special dialectic forms or otherwise peculiar linguistic patterns are common among primitive peoples for the texts of songs. Sometimes, as in Melanesia, such song texts are due to the influence of neighboring dialects. This is strangely analogous to the practice among ourselves of singing songs in Italian, French, or German rather than in English, and it is likely that the historical processes which have led to the parallel custom are of a similar nature. Thieves' jargon and secret languages of children may also be mentioned. These lead over into special sign and gesture languages, many of which are based directly on spoken or written speech; they seem to exist on many levels of culture. The sign language of the Plains Indians of North America arose in response to the need for some medium of communication between tribes speaking mutually unintelligible languages. Within the Christian church we may note the elaboration of gesture languages by orders of monks vowed to silence.

Not only a language or a terminology but the mere external form in which it is written may become important as a symbol of sentimental or social distinction. Thus Croatian and Serbian are essentially the same language but they are presented in very different outward forms, the former being written in Latin characters, the latter in the Cyrillic character of the Greek Orthodox church. This external difference, associated with a difference in religion, has of course the important function of preventing people who speak closely related languages or dialects but who wish for reasons of sentiment not to confound themselves in a larger unity from becoming too keenly aware of how much they actually resemble each other.

The relation of language to nationalism and internationalism presents a number of interesting sociological problems. Anthropology makes a rigid distinction between ethnic units based on race, on culture, and on language. It points out that these do not need to coincide in the least—that they do not, as a matter of fact, often coincide in reality. But with the increased emphasis on nationalism in modern times, the question of the symbolic meaning of race and language has taken on a new significance and, whatever the scientist may say, the layman is ever inclined to see culture, language, and race as but different facets of a single social unity which he tends in turn to identify with such political entities as England or France or Germany. To point out, as the anthropologist easily can, that cultural distributions and nationalities override language and race groups, does not end the matter for the sociologist, because he feels that the concept of nation or nationality must be integrally imaged in behavior by the non-analytical person as carrying with it the connotation, real or supposed, of both race and language. From this standpoint it really makes little difference whether history and anthropology support the popular identification of nationality, language, and race. The important thing to hold on to is that a particular language tends to become the fitting expression of a self-conscious nationality and that such a group will construct for itself, in spite of all that the physical anthropologist can do, a race to which is to be attributed the mystic power of creating a language and a culture as twin expressions of its psychic peculiarities.

So far as language and race are concerned, it is true that the major races of man have tended in the past to be set off against each other by important differences of language. There is less point to this, however, than might be imagined, because the linguistic differentiations within any given race are just as far-reaching as those which can be pointed out across racial lines, yet they do not at all correspond to sub-racial units. Even the major races are not always clearly sundered by language. This is notably the case with the Malayo-Polynesian languages, which are spoken by peoples as racially distinct as the Malays, the Polynesians, and the Negroes of Melanesia. Not one of the great languages of modern man follows racial lines. French, for example, is spoken by a highly mixed population which is largely Nordic in the north, Alpine in the center, and Mediterranean in the south, each of these subraces being liberally represented in the rest of Europe.

While language differences have always been important symbols of cultural difference, it is only in comparatively recent times, with the exaggerated development of the ideal of the sovereign nation and with the resulting eagerness to discover linguistic symbols for this ideal of sovereignty, that language differences have taken on an implication of antagonism. In ancient Rome and all through mediaeval Europe there were plenty of cultural differences running side by side with linguistic ones, and the political status of Roman citizen or the fact of adherence to the Roman Catholic church was of vastly greater significance as a symbol of the individual's place in the world than the language or dialect he happened to speak. It is probably altogether incorrect to maintain that language differences are responsible for national antagonisms. It would seem to be much more reasonable to suppose that a political and national unit, once definitely formed, uses a prevailing language as a symbol of its identity, whence gradually emerges the peculiarly modern feeling that every language should properly be the expression of a distinctive nationality.

In earlier times there seems to have been little systematic attempt to impose the language of a conquering people on the subject people, although it happened frequently as a result of the processes implicit in the spread of culture that such a conqueror's language was gradually taken over by the dispossessed population. Witness the spread of the Romance languages and of the modern Arabic dialects. On the other hand, it seems to have happened about as frequently that the conquering group was culturally and linguistically absorbed and that their own language disappeared without necessary danger to their privileged status. Thus foreign dynasties in China have always submitted to the superior culture of the Chinese and have taken on their language. In the same way the Moslem Moguls of India, while true to their religion, made one of the Hindu vernaculars the basis of the great literary language of Moslem India, Hindustani. Definitely repressive attitudes toward the languages and dialects of subject peoples seem to be distinctive only of European political policy in comparatively recent times. The attempt of czarist Russia to stamp out Polish by forbidding its teaching in the schools and the similarly repressive policy of contemporary Italy in its attempt to wipe out German from the territory recently acquired from Austria are illuminating examples of the heightened emphasis on language as a symbol of political allegiance in the modern world.

To match these repressive measures, we have the oft repeated attempt of minority groups to erect their language into the status of a fully accredited medium of cultural and literary expression. Many of these restored or semimanufactured languages have come in on the wave of resistance to political or cultural hostility. Such are the Gaelic of Ireland, the Lithuanian of a recently created republic, and the Hebrew of the Zionists. Other such languages have come in more peacefully because of a sentimental interest in local culture. Such are the modern Provençal of southern France, the Plattdeutsch of northern Germany, Frisian, and the Norwegian *landsmaal*. It is very doubtful whether these persistent attempts to make true culture languages of local dialects that have long ceased to be of primary literary importance can succeed in the long run. The failure of modern Provençal to hold its own and the very dubious success of Gaelic make it seem probable that, following the recent tendency to resurrect minor languages, there will come a renewed leveling of speech more suitably expressing the internationalism which is slowly emerging.

The logical necessity of an international language in modern times is in strange contrast to the indif-

ference and even opposition with which most people
consider its possibility. The attempts so far made to
solve this problem, of which Esperanto has probably
had the greatest measure of practical success, have
not affected more than a very small proportion of the
people whose international interest and needs might
have led to a desire for a simple and uniform means
of international expression, at least for certain purposes. It is in the less important countries of Europe,
such as Czechoslovakia, that Esperanto has been
moderately successful, and for obvious reasons.

The opposition to an international language has
little logic or psychology in its favor. The supposed
artificiality of such a language as Esperanto or any
of the equivalent languages that have been proposed
is absurdly exaggerated, for in sober truth there is
practically nothing in these languages that is not
taken from the common stock of words and forms
which have gradually developed in Europe. Such an
international language could, of course, have only
the status of a secondary form of speech for distinctly
limited purposes. Thus considered, the learning of a
constructed international language offers no further
psychological problem than the learning of any other
language which is acquired after childhood through
the medium of books and with the conscious application of grammatical rules. The lack of interest in
the international language problem in spite of the
manifest need for one is an excellent example of how
little logic or intellectual necessity has to do with the
acquirement of language habits. Even the acquiring
of the barest smattering of a foreign language is

imaginatively equivalent to some measure of identification with a people or a culture. The purely instrumental value of such knowledge is frequently nil.

Any consciously constructed international language has to deal with the great difficulty of not being felt to represent a distinctive people or culture. Hence the learning of it is of very little symbolic significance for the average person, who remains blind to the fact that such a language, easy and regular as it inevitably must be, would solve many of his educational and practical difficulties at a single blow. The future alone will tell whether the logical advantages and theoretical necessity of an international language can overcome the largely symbolic opposition which it has to meet. In any event it is at least conceivable that one of the great national languages of modern times, such as English or Spanish or Russian, may in due course find itself in the position of a *de facto* international language without any conscious attempt having been made to put it there.

The Function of an International Auxiliary Language

As to the theoretical desirability of an international auxiliary language there can be little difference of opinion. As to just what factors in the solution of the problem should be allowed to weigh most heavily there is room for every possible difference of opinion, and so it is not surprising that interlinguists are far from having reached complete agreement as to either method or content. So far as the advocates of a constructed international language are concerned, it is rather to be wondered at how much in common their proposals actually have, both in vocabulary and in general spirit of procedure. The crucial differences of opinion lie not so much between one constructed language and another as between the idea of a constructed language and that of an already well-established national one, whether in its traditional, authorized form or in some simplified form of it. It is not uncommon to hear it said by those who stand somewhat outside the international language question that some such regular system as Esperanto is

Psyche, vol. 11, no. 4 (1931), pp. 4–15. Also published in H. N. Shenton, E. Sapir, and O. Jespersen, *International Communication: A Symposium on the Language Problem* (London, 1931), pp. 65–94.

theoretically desirable but that it is of little use to work for it because English is already *de facto* the international language of modern times—if not altogether at the moment, then in the immediate future —that English is simple enough and regular enough to satisfy all practical requirements, and that the precise form of it as an international language may well be left to historical and psychological factors that one need not worry about in advance. This point of view has a certain pleasing plausibility about it but, like so many things that seem plausible and effortless, it may none the less embody a number of fallacies.

It is the purpose of this paper to try to clarify the fundamental question of what is to be expected of an international auxiliary language, and whether the explicit and tacit requirements can be better satisfied by a constructed language or by a national language, including some simplified version of it. I believe that much of the difficulty in the international language question lies precisely in lack of clarity as to these fundamental functions.

There are two considerations, often intermingled in practice, which arouse the thought of an international language. The first is the purely practical problem of facilitating the growing need for international communication in its most elementary sense. A firm, for instance, that does business in many countries of the world is driven to spend an enormous amount of time, labour, and money in providing for translation services. From a purely technological point of view, all this is sheer waste, and while one accepts the necessity of going to all the linguistic trouble that the expansion of trade demands, one does so with something like a shrug of the shoulder. One speaks of a 'necessary evil.' Again, at an international scientific meeting one is invariably disappointed to find that the primary difficulty of communicating with foreign scientists because of differences of language habits makes it not so easy to exchange ideas of moment as one had fantasied might be the case before setting sail. Here again one speaks of a 'necessary evil,' and comforts oneself with the reflection that if the scientific ideas which it was not too easy to follow at the meeting are of moment they will, sooner or later, be presented in cold print, so that nothing is essentially lost. One can always congratulate oneself on having had an interesting time and on having made some charming personal contacts. Such examples can, of course, be multiplied *ad infinitum*. Too much is not made, as a rule, of any specific difficulty in linguistic communication, but the cumulative effect of these difficulties is stupendous in magnitude. Sooner or later one chafes and begins to wonder whether the evil is as 'necessary' as tradition would have it. Impatience translates itself into a desire to have something immediate done about it all, and, as is generally the case with impatience, resolves itself in the easiest way that lies ready to hand. Why not push English, for instance, which is already spoken over a larger area than any other language of modern times, and which shows every sign of spreading in the world of commerce and travel? The consideration which gives rise to reflections of this sort, grounded in impatience as it

is, looks for no more worthy solution of the difficulty
than a sort of minimum language, a *lingua franca* of
the modern world. Those who argue in this spirit invariably pride themselves on being 'practical,' and,
like all 'practical' people, they are apt to argue without their host.

The opposed consideration is not as easy to state
and can be so stated as to seem to be identical with
the first. It should be put in something like the following form: An international auxiliary language
should serve as a broad base for every type of international understanding, which means, of course, in
the last analysis, for every type of expression of the
human spirit which is of more than local interest,
which in turn can be restated so as to include any
and all human interests. The exigencies of trade or
travel are from this point of view merely some of
the more obvious symptoms of the internationalizing
of the human mind, and it would be a mistake to expect too little of an organ of international expression.
But this is not all. The modern mind tends to be
more and more critical and analytical in spirit, hence
it must devise for itself an engine of expression which
is logically defensible at every point and which tends
to correspond to the rigorous spirit of modern science. This does not mean that a constructed international language is expected to have the perfection
of mathematical symbolism, but it must be progressively felt as moving in that direction. Perhaps the
speakers of a national language are under profound
illusions as to the logical character of its structure.
Perhaps they confuse the comfort of habit with logi-

cal necessity. If this is so—and I do not see how it can be seriously doubted that it is—it must mean that in the long run the modern spirit will not rest satisfied with an international language that merely extends the imperfections and provincialisms of one language at the expense of all others.

These two opposing considerations seem to me to be the primary ones. They may be rephrased as "what can be done right now" and "what should be done in the long run." There are also other considerations that are of importance, and among them perhaps the most obvious is the attitude of people toward the spread or imposition of any national language which is not their own. The psychology of a language which, in one way or another, is imposed upon one because of factors beyond one's control, is very different from the psychology of a language that one accepts of one's free will. In a sense, every form of expression is imposed upon one by social factors, one's own language above all. But it is the thought or illusion of freedom that is the important thing, not the fact of it. The modern world is confronted by the difficulty of reconciling internationalism with its persistent and tightening nationalisms. More and more, unsolicited gifts from without are likely to be received with unconscious resentment. Only that can be freely accepted which is in some sense a creation of all. A common creation demands a common sacrifice, and perhaps not the least potent argument in favour of a constructed international language is the fact that it is equally foreign, or apparently so, to the traditions of all nationalities. The

common difficulty gives it an impersonal character
and silences the resentment that is born of rivalry.
English, once accepted as an international language,
is no more secure than French has proved to be as
the one and only accepted language of diplomacy
or as Latin has proved to be as the international language of science. Both French and Latin are involved with nationalistic and religious implications
which could not be entirely shaken off, and so, while
they seemed for a long time to have solved the international language problem up to a certain point,
they did not really do so in spirit. English would
probably fare no better, and it is even likely that the
tradition of trade, finance, and superficial practicality
in general that attaches to English may, in the long
run, prove more of a hindrance than a help to the
unreserved acceptance of English as an adequate
means of international expression One must beware
of an over-emphasis on the word 'auxiliary.' It is perfectly true that for untold generations to come an
international language must be auxiliary, must not
attempt to set itself up against the many languages
of the folk, but it must for all that be a free powerful
expression of its own, capable of all work that may
reasonably be expected of language and protected
by the powerful negative fact that it cannot be interpreted as the symbol of any localism or nationality.

Whether or not some national language, say, English, or a constructed language, say Esperanto, is to
win out in the immediate future, does not depend
primarily on conscious forces that can be manipu-
lated, but on many obscure and impersonal political,

economic and social determinants. One can only hope that one senses the more significant of these determinants and helps along with such efforts as one can master. Even if it be assumed for the sake of argument that English is to spread as an auxiliary language over the whole world, it does not in the least follow that the international language problem is disposed of. English, or some simplified version of it, may spread for certain immediate and practical purposes, yet the deeper needs of the modern world may not be satisfied by it and we may still have to deal with a conflict between an English that has won a too easy triumph and a constructed language that has such obvious advantages of structure that it may gradually displace its national rival.

What is needed above all is a language that is as simple, as regular, as logical, as rich, and as creative as possible; a language which starts with a minimum of demands on the learning capacity of the normal individual and can do the maximum amount of work; which is to serve as a sort of logical touchstone to all national languages and as the standard medium of translation. It must, ideally, be as superior to any accepted language as the mathematical method of expressing quantities and relations between quantities is to the more lumbering methods of expressing these quantities and relations in verbal form. This is undoubtedly an ideal which can never be reached, but ideals are not meant to be reached: they merely indicate the direction of movement.

I spoke before about the illusions that the average man has about the nature of his own language. It will help to clarify matters if we take a look at English from the standpoint of simplicity, regularity, logic, richness, and creativeness. We may begin with simplicity. It is true that English is not as complex in its formal structure as is German or Latin, but this does not dispose of the matter. The fact that a beginner in English has not many paradigms to learn gives him a feeling of absence of difficulty, but he soon learns to his cost that this is only a feeling, that in sober fact the very absence of explicit guide-posts to structure leads him into all sorts of quandaries. A few examples will be useful. One of the glories of English simplicity is the possibility of using the same word as noun and verb. We speak, for instance, of "having cut the meat" and of "a cut of meat." We not only "kick a person," but "give him a kick." One may either "ride horseback" or "take a ride." At first blush this looks like a most engaging rule but a little examination convinces us that the supposed simplicity of word-building is a mirage. In the first place, in what sense may a verb be used as a noun? In the case of "taking a ride" or "giving a kick" the noun evidently indicates the act itself. In the case of "having a cut on the head" or "eating a cut of meat," it just as clearly does not indicate the act itself but the result of the act, and these two examples do not even illustrate the same kind of result, for in the former case the cut is conceived of as the wound that results from cutting, whereas in the latter case it refers to the portion of meat which is loosened by the act of cutting. Anyone who takes the trouble to examine these examples carefully will soon see that be-

hind a superficial appearance of simplicity there is
concealed a perfect hornet's nest of bizarre and arbitrary usages. To those of us who speak English
from the earliest years of our childhood these difficulties do not readily appear. To one who comes to
English from a language which possesses a totally
different structure such facts as these are disconcert-
ing. But there is a second difficulty with the rule, or
tendency, which allows us to use the unmodified
verb as a noun. Not only is the function of the noun
obscure, but in a great many cases we cannot use
it at all, or the usage is curiously restricted. We can
"give a person a shove" or "a push," but we cannot
"give him a move" nor "a drop" (in the sense of caus-
ing him to drop). We can "give one help," but we
"give obedience," not "obey." A complete examination, in short, of all cases in which the verb functions
as a noun would disclose two exceedingly cheerless
facts: that there is a considerable number of distinct
senses in which the verb may be so employed,
though no rule can be given as to which of these possible senses is the proper one in any particular case
or whether only one or more than one such meaning
is possible; and that in many cases no such nouns
may be formed at all, but that either nouns of an entirely different formation must be used or else that
they are not possible at all. We thus have to
set up such rather cranky-looking configurations as

$$\text{to help:help} = \text{to obey:obedience}$$
$$= \text{to grow:growth}$$
$$= \text{to drown:drowning,}$$

a set-up which is further complicated by the fact that such a word as 'drowning' not only corresponds to such words as 'help' and 'growth,' but also to such words as 'helping' and 'growing.' The precise disentanglement of all these relations and the obtaining of anything like assurance in the use of the words is a task of no small difficulty. Where, then, is the simplicity with which we started? It is obviously a phantom. The English-speaking person covers up the difficulty for himself by speaking vaguely of idioms. The real point is that behind the vagaries of idiomatic usage there are perfectly clear-cut logical relations which are only weakly brought out in the overt form of English. The simplicity of English in its formal aspect is, therefore, really a pseudo-simplicity or a masked complexity.

Another example of apparent, but only apparent, simplicity in English is the use of such vague verbs as 'to put' and 'to get.' To us the verb 'put' is a very simple matter, both in form and in use. Actually it is an amazingly difficult word to learn to use and no rules can be given either for its employment or for its avoidance. 'To put at rest' gives us an impression of simplicity because of the overt simplicity of the structure, but here again the simplicity is an illusion. 'To put at rest' really means 'to cause to rest,' and its apparent analogy to such constructions as 'to put it at a great distance,' so far from helping thought, really hinders it, for the formal analogy is not paralleled by a conceptual one. 'To put out of danger' is formally analogous to 'to put out of school,' but here too the analogy is utterly misleading, un-

less, indeed, one defines school as a form of danger.
If we were to define 'put' as a kind of causative op-
erator, we should get into trouble, for it cannot be
safely used as such in all cases. In such a sentence
as "The ship put to sea," for example, there is no implied causative relation. If English cannot give the
foreigner clear rules for the employment of verbs as
nouns or for such apparently simple verbs as 'put,'
what advantage is derived by him from the merely
negative fact that he has not much formal grammar
to learn in these cases? He may well feel that the apparent simplicity of English is purchased at the price
of a bewildering obscurity. He may even feel that the
mastery of English usage is, in the long run, much
more difficult than the application of a fairly large
number of rules for the formation of words, so long
as these rules are unambiguous.

English has no monopoly of pseudo-simplicity.
French and German illustrate the misleading character of apparent grammatical simplicity just as well.
One example from French will serve our purpose.
There is no doubt that the French speaker feels that
he has in the reflexive verb a perfectly simple and, on
the whole, unambiguous form of expression. A logical
analysis of reflexive usages in French shows, however,
that this simplicity is an illusion and that, so far from
helping the foreigner, it is more calculated to bother
him. In some cases the French reflexive is a true reflexive; that is, it indicates that the subject of the sentence is the same as the object. An example of a
reflexive verb of this sort would be *se tuer*, 'to kill
oneself.' To French feeling this sort of verb is doubt-

less identical with the type illustrated by *s'amuser*.
Logically, however, one does not 'amuse oneself' in
the sense in which one 'kills oneself.' The possibility
of translating 'to amuse oneself' into 'to have a good
time' and the impossibility of translating 'to kill oneself' into 'to have a bad time killing,' or something of
that sort, at once shows the weakness of the analogy.
Logically, of course, *s'amuser* is not a true reflexive at
all, but merely an intransitive verb of the same general type as 'to rejoice' or 'to laugh' or 'to play.' Furthermore, the French verb *se battre* gives the Frenchman precisely the same formal feeling as *se tuer* and
s'amuser. Actually it is a reciprocal verb which may
be translated as 'to strike one another' and, therefore, 'to fight.' Finally, in such a verb as *s'étendre*,
'to extend' or 'to stretch,' the Frenchman distinctly
feels the reflexive force, the stretching of the road, for
instance, being conceived of as a self-stretching of the
road, as though the road took itself and lengthened
itself out. This type of verb may be called a pseudo-
reflexive, or a non-agentive active verb, the point being that the action, while of a type that is generally
brought about by an outside agency, is conceived of
as taking place without definite agency. In English,
verbs of this kind are regularly used without the reflexive, as in 'the road stretches,' 'the string breaks,'
'the rag tears,' 'the bag bursts,' which are the
non-agentive correspondents of such usages as 'he
stretches the rubber band,' 'he breaks the string,' 'he
tears the rag,' 'he bursts the balloon.' It should be
clear that a linguistic usage, such as the French reflexive, which throws together four such logically

distinct categories as the true reflexive, the simple intransitive, the reciprocal, and the non-agentive active, purchases simplicity at a considerable price. For the Frenchman such usage is convenient enough and no ambiguity seems to result. But for the outsider, who comes to French with a different alignment of forms in his mind, the simplicity that is offered is puzzling and treacherous.

These examples of the lack of simplicity in English and French, all appearances to the contrary, could be multiplied almost without limit and apply to all national languages. In fact, one may go so far as to say that it is precisely the apparent simplicity of structure which is suggested by the formal simplicity of many languages which is responsible for much slovenliness in thought, and even for the creation of imaginary problems in philosophy. What has been said of simplicity applies equally to regularity and logic, as some of our examples have already indicated. No important national language, at least in the Occidental world, has complete regularity of grammatical structure, nor is there a single logical category which is adequately and consistently handled in terms of linguistic symbolism. It is well known that the tense systems of French, English and German teem with logical inconsistencies as they are actually used. Many categories which are of great logical and psychological importance are so haltingly expressed that it takes a good deal of effort to prove to the average man that they exist at all. A good example of such a category is that of 'aspect,' in the technical sense of the word. Few English-speaking people see such a locution as 'to burst into tears' or 'to burst out laughing' as much more than an idiomatic oddity. As a matter of fact, English is here trying to express, as best it can, an intuition of the 'momentaneous aspect'; in other words, of activity seen as a point in contrast to activity seen as a line. Logically and psychologically, nearly every activity can be thought of as either point-like or line-like in character, and there are, of course, many expressions in English which definitely point to the one or to the other, but the treatment of these intuitions is fragmentary and illogical throughout.

A standard international language should not only be simple, regular, and logical, but also rich and creative. Richness is a difficult and subjective concept. It would, of course, be hopeless to attempt to crowd into an international language all those local overtones of meaning which are so dear to the heart of the nationalist. There is a growing fund of common experience and sentiment which will have to be expressed in an international language, and it would be strange if the basic fund of meanings would not grow in richness with the interactions of human beings who make use of the international medium. The supposed inferiority of a constructed language to a national one on the score of richness of connotation is, of course, no criticism of the idea of a constructed language. All that the criticism means is that the constructed language has not been in long-continued use. As a matter of fact, a national language which spreads beyond its own confines very quickly loses much of its original richness of content and is in no better case than a constructed language.

More important is the question of creativeness. Here there are many illusions. All languages, even the most primitive, have very real powers of creating new words and combinations of words as they are needed, but the theoretical possibilities of creation are in most of these national languages which are of importance for the international language question thwarted by all sorts of irrelevant factors that would not apply to a constructed language. English, for instance, has a great many formal resources at its disposal which it seems unable to use adequately; for instance, there is no reason why the suffix -*ness* should not be used to make up an unlimited number of words indicating quality, such as 'smallness' and 'opaqueness,' yet we know that only a limited number of such forms is possible. One says 'width,' not 'wideness'; 'beauty,' not 'beautifulness.' In the same way, such locutions as 'to give a kick' and 'to give a slap' might be supposed to serve as models for the creation of an unlimited number of momentaneous verbs, yet the possibilities of extending this form of usage are strictly limited. The truth is that sentiment and precedent prevent the national language, with its accepted tradition, from doing all it might do, and the logically possible formations of all kinds which would be felt as awkward or daring in English, or even in German, could be accepted as the merest matters of course in an international language that was not tied to the dictates of irrational usage.

We see, then, that no national language really corresponds in spirit to the analytic and creative spirit of modern times. National languages are all huge systems of vested interests which sullenly resist critical inquiry. It may shock the traditionalist to be told that we are rapidly getting to the point where our national languages are almost more of a hindrance than a help to clear thinking; yet how true this is is significantly illustrated by the necessity that mathematics and symbolic logic have been under of developing their own systems of symbolism. There is a perfectly obvious objection that is often raised at this point. We are told that normal human expression does not crave any such accuracy as is attained by these rigorous disciplines. True, but it is not a question of remodeling language in the spirit of mathematics and symbolic logic, but merely of giving it the structural means whereby it may refine itself in as economical and unambiguous a manner as possible.

It is likely that the foundations of a truly adequate form of international language have already been laid in Esperanto and other proposed international auxiliary languages, but it is doubtful if the exacting ideal that we have sketched is attained by any one of them, or is likely to be attained for some time to come. It is, therefore, highly desirable that along with the practical labour of getting wider recognition of the international language idea, there go hand in hand comparative researches which aim to lay bare the logical structures that are inadequately symbolized in our present-day languages, in order that we may see more clearly than we have yet been able to see just how much of psychological insight and logical rigour have been and can be expressed in linguistic form. One of the most ambitious and important tasks that can be undertaken is the attempt to work out the relation between logic and usage in a number of national and constructed languages, in order that the eventual problem of adequately symbolizing thought may be seen as the problem it still is. No doubt it will be impossible, for a long time to come, to give a definite answer to all of the questions that are raised, but it is something to raise and define the questions.

I have emphasized the logical advantages of a constructed international language, but it is important not to neglect the psychological ones. The attitude of independence toward a constructed language which all national speakers must adopt is really a great advantage, because it tends to make man see himself as the master of language instead of its obedient servant. A common allegiance to form of expression that is identified with no single national unit is likely to prove one of the most potent symbols of the freedom of the human spirit that the world has yet known. As the Oriental peoples become of more and more importance in the modern world, the air of sanctity that attaches to English or German or French is likely to seem less and less a thing to be taken for granted, and it is not at all unlikely that the eventual triumph of the international language movement will owe much to the Chinaman's and the Indian's indifference to the vested interests of Europe, though the actual stock of basic words in any prac-

tical international language is almost certain to be
based on the common European fund. A further psychological advantage of a constructed language has
been often referred to by those who have had experience with such languages as Esperanto. This is the
removal of fear in the public use of a language other
than one's native tongue. The use of the wrong gender in French or any minor violence to English idiom
is construed as a sin of etiquette, and everyone knows
how paralyzing on freedom of expression is the fear
of committing the slightest breach of etiquette. Who
knows to what extent the discreet utterances of foreign visitors are really due to their wise unwillingness
to take too many chances with the vagaries of a foreign language? It is, of course, not the language as
such which is sinned against, but the conventions of
fitness which are in the minds of the natives who act
as custodians of the language. Expression in a constructed language has no such fears as these to reckon
with. Errors in Esperanto speech are not sins or
breaches of etiquette; they are merely trivialities to
the extent that they do not actually misrepresent the
meaning of the speaker, and as such they may be ignored.

In the educational world there is a great deal of dis-
content with the teaching of classical and modern
languages. It is no secret that the fruits of language
study are in no sort of relation to the labour spent on
teaching and learning them. Who has not the uncomfortable feeling that there is something intellectually dishonest about a course of study that goes in for
half-hearted tinkering with, say, Latin and two mod-

ern languages, with a net result that is more or less microscopic in value? A feeling is growing that the study of foreign languages should be relegated to the class of technical specialties and that the efforts of educators should be directed rather toward deepening the conceptual language sense of students in order that, thus equipped, they may as occasion arises be in a better position to learn what national languages they may happen to need. A well-constructed international language is much more easily learned than a national language, sharpens one's insight into the logical structure of expression in a way that none of these does, and puts one in possession of a great deal of lexical material which can be turned to account in the analysis of both the speaker's language and of most others that he is likely to want to learn. Certain beginnings have already been made toward the adoption of international language study as a means toward general language work. Time alone can tell whether this movement is a fruitful one, but it is certainly an aspect of the international language question that is worth thinking about, particularly in America, with its growing impatience of the largely useless teaching of Latin, French, German, and Spanish in the high schools. The international language movement has had, up to the present time, a somewhat cliquish or esoteric air. It now looks as though it might take on the characteristics of an international Open Forum. The increasing degree to which linguists, mathematicians and scientists have been thinking about the problem is a sign that promises well for the future. It is a good thing that the idea of an international language is no longer presented in merely idealistic terms, but is more and more taking on the aspect of a practical or technological problem and of an exercise in the cleaning up of the thought process. Intelligent men should not allow themselves to become international language doctrinaires. They should do all they can to keep the problem experimental, welcoming criticism at every point and trusting to the gradual emergence of an international language that is a fit medium for the modern spirit.

The spirit of logical analysis should in practice blend with the practical pressure for the adoption of some form of international language, but it should not allow itself to be stampeded by it. It would be exceedingly unfortunate if an international language, whether Esperanto or English or some form of simplified English, were looked upon as thenceforth sacred and inviolate. No solution of the international language problem should be looked upon as more than a beginning toward the gradual evolution, in the light of experience and at the hand of all civilized humanity, of an international language which is as rich as any now known to us, is far more creative in its possibilities, and is infinitely simpler, more regular, and more logical than any one of them.

The Status of Linguistics as a Science

Linguistics may be said to have begun its scientific career with the comparative study and reconstruction of the Indo-European languages. In the course of their detailed researches Indo-European linguists have gradually developed a technique which is probably more nearly perfect than that of any other science dealing with man's institutions. Many of the formulations of comparative Indo-European linguistics have a neatness and a regularity which recall the formulae, or the so-called laws, of natural science. Historical and comparative linguistics has been built up chiefly on the basis of the hypothesis that sound changes are regular and that most morphological readjustments in language follow as by-products in the wake of these regular phonetic developments. There are many who would be disposed to deny the psychological necessity of the regularity of sound change, but it remains true, as a matter of actual linguistic experience, that faith in such regularity has been the most successful approach to the historic

Language, vol. 5 (1929), 207–214. Read at a joint meeting of the Linguistic Society of America, the American Anthropological Association, and Sections H and L of the American Association for the Advancement of Science, New York City, December 28, 1928.

problems of language. Why such regularities should be found and why it is necessary to assume regularity of sound change are questions that the average linguist is perhaps unable to answer satisfactorily. But it does not follow that he can expect to improve his methods by discarding well tested hypotheses and throwing the field open to all manner of psychological and sociological explanations that do not immediately tie up with what we actually know about the historical behavior of language. A psychological and a sociological interpretation of the kind of regularity in linguistic change with which students of language have long been familiar are indeed desirable and even necessary. But neither psychology nor sociology is in a position to tell linguistics what kinds of historical formulations the linguist is to make. At best these disciplines can but urge the linguist to concern himself in a more vital manner than heretofore with the problem of seeing linguistic history in the larger framework of human behavior in the individual and in society.

The methods developed by the Indo-Europeanists have been applied with marked success to other groups of languages. It is abundantly clear that they apply just as rigorously to the unwritten primitive languages of Africa and America as to the better known forms of speech of the more sophisticated peoples. It is probably in the languages of these more cultured peoples that the fundamental regularity of linguistic processes has been most often crossed by the operation of such conflicting tendencies as borrowing from other languages, dialectic blending, and social differentiations of speech. The more we devote ourselves to the comparative study of the languages of a primitive linguistic stock, the more clearly we realize that phonetic law and analogical leveling are the only satisfactory key to the unravelling of the development of dialects and languages from a common base. Professor Leonard Bloomfield's experiences with Central Algonkian and my own with Athabaskan leave nothing to be desired in this respect and are a complete answer to those who find it difficult to accept the large-scale regularity of the operation of all those unconscious linguistic forces which in their totality give us regular phonetic change and morphological readjustment on the basis of such change. It is not merely theoretically possible to predict the correctness of specific forms among unlettered peoples on the basis of such phonetic laws as have been worked out for them—such predictions are already on record in considerable number. There can be no doubt that the methods first developed in the field of Indo-European linguistics are destined to play a consistently important rôle in the study of all other groups of languages, and that it is through them and through their gradual extension that we can hope to arrive at significant historical inferences as to the remoter relations between groups of languages that show few superficial signs of a common origin.

It is the main purpose of this paper, however, not to insist on what linguistics has already accomplished, but rather to point out some of the connections between linguistics and other scientific disciplines, and above all to raise the question in what sense linguistics can be called a 'science.'

The value of linguistics for anthropology and culture history has long been recognized. As linguistic research has proceeded, language has proved useful as a tool in the sciences of man and has itself required and obtained a great deal of light from the rest of these sciences. It is difficult for a modern linguist to confine himself to his traditional subject matter. Unless he is somewhat unimaginative, he cannot but share in some or all of the mutual interests which tie up linguistics with anthropology and culture history, with sociology, with psychology, with philosophy, and, more remotely, with physics and physiology.

Language is becoming increasingly valuable as a guide to the scientific study of a given culture. In a sense, the network of cultural patterns of a civilization is indexed in the language which expresses that civilization. It is an illusion to think that we can understand the significant outlines of a culture through sheer observation and without the guide of the linguistic symbolism which makes these outlines significant and intelligible to society. Some day the attempt to master a primitive culture without the help of the language of its society will seem as amateurish as the labors of a historian who cannot handle the original documents of the civilization which he is describing.

Language is a guide to 'social reality.' Though language is not ordinarily thought of as of essential interest to the students of social science, it powerfully conditions all our thinking about social problems and processes. Human beings do not live in the objective world alone, nor alone in the world of social activity as ordinarily understood, but are very much at the mercy of the particular language which has become the medium of expression for their society. It is quite an illusion to imagine that one adjusts to reality essentially without the use of language and that language is merely an incidental means of solving specific problems of communication or reflection. The fact of the matter is that the 'real world' is to a large extent unconsciously built up on the language habits of the group. No two languages are ever sufficiently similar to be considered as representing the same social reality. The worlds in which different societies live are distinct worlds, not merely the same world with different labels attached.

The understanding of a simple poem, for instance, involves not merely an understanding of the single words in their average significance, but a full comprehension of the whole life of the community as it is mirrored in the words, or as it is suggested by their overtones. Even comparatively simple acts of perception are very much more at the mercy of the social patterns called words than we might suppose. If one draws some dozen lines, for instance, of different shapes, one perceives them as divisible into such categories as 'straight,' 'crooked,' 'curved,' 'zigzag' because of the classificatory suggestiveness of the linguistic terms themselves. We see and hear and otherwise experience very largely as we do because the language habits of our community predispose certain choices of interpretation.

For the more fundamental problems of the student of human culture, therefore, a knowledge of linguistic mechanisms and historical developments is certain to become more and more important as our analysis of social behavior becomes more refined. From this standpoint we may think of language as the *symbolic guide to culture.* In another sense too linguistics is of great assistance in the study of cultural phenomena. Many cultural objects and ideas have been diffused in connection with their terminology, so that a study of the distribution of culturally significant terms often throws unexpected light on the history of inventions and ideas. This type of research, already fruitful in European and Asiatic culture history, is destined to be of great assistance in the reconstruction of primitive cultures.

The values of linguistics for sociology in the narrower sense of the word is just as real as for the anthropological theorist. Sociologists are necessarily interested in the technique of communication between human beings. From this standpoint language facilitation and language barriers are of the utmost importance and must be studied in their interplay with a host of other factors that make for ease or difficulty of transmission of ideas and patterns of behavior. Furthermore, the sociologist is necessarily interested in the symbolic significance, in a social sense, of the linguistic differences which appear in any large community. Correctness of speech or what might be called 'social style' in speech is of far more than aesthetic or grammatical interest. Peculiar modes of pronunciation, characteristic turns of phrase, slangy forms of speech, occupational terminologies of all sorts—these are so many symbols of the manifold ways in which society arranges itself and are of crucial importance for the understanding of the development of individual and social attitudes. Yet it will not be possible for a social student to evaluate such phenomena unless he has very clear notions of the linguistic background against which social symbolisms of a linguistic sort are to be estimated.

It is very encouraging that the psychologist has been concerning himself more and more with linguistic data. So far it is doubtful if he has been able to contribute very much to the understanding of language behavior beyond what the linguist has himself been able to formulate on the basis of his data. But the feeling is growing rapidly, and justly, that the psychological explanations of the linguists themselves need to be restated in more general terms, so that purely linguistic facts may be seen as specialized forms of symbolic behavior. The psychologists have perhaps too narrowly concerned themselves with the simple psycho-physical bases of speech and have not penetrated very deeply into the study of its symbolic nature. This is probably due to the fact that psychologists in general are as yet too little aware of the fundamental importance of symbolism in behavior. It is not unlikely that it is precisely in the field of symbolism that linguistic forms and processes will contribute most to the enrichment of psychology.

All activities may be thought of as either definitely

functional in the immediate sense, or as symbolic, or
as a blend of the two. Thus, if I shove open a door in
order to enter a house, the significance of the act lies
precisely in its allowing me to make an easy entry.
But if I 'knock at the door,' a little reflection shows
that the knock in itself does not open the door for
me. It serves merely as a sign that somebody is to
come to open it for me. To knock on the door is a
substitute for the more primitive act of shoving it
open of one's own accord. We have here the rudi-
ments of what might be called language. A vast
number of acts are language acts in this crude sense.
That is, they are not of importance to us because of
the work they immediately do, but because they
serve as mediating signs of other more important
acts. A primitive sign has some objective resemblance
to what it takes the place of or points to. Thus,
knocking at the door has a definite relation to in-
tended activity upon the door itself. Some signs become abbreviated forms of functional activities which
can be used for reference. Thus, shaking one's fist at
a person is an abbreviated and relatively harmless
way of actually punching him. If such a gesture becomes sufficiently expressive to society to constitute
in some sort the equivalent of an abuse or a threat,
it may be looked on as a symbol in the proper sense
of the word.

Symbols of this sort are primary in that the resemblance of the symbol to what it stands for is still
fairly evident. As time goes on, symbols become so
completely changed in form as to lose all outward
connection with what they stand for. Thus, there is

no resemblance between a piece of bunting colored red, white, and blue, and the United States of America—itself a complex and not easily definable notion. The flag may therefore be looked upon as a secondary or referential symbol. The way to understand language psychologically, it seems, is to see it as the most complicated example of such a secondary or referential set of symbols that society has evolved. It may be that originally the primal cries or other types of symbols developed by man had some connection with certain emotions or attitudes or notions. But a connection is no longer directly traceable between words, or combinations of words, and what they refer to.

Linguistics is at once one of the most difficult and one of the most fundamental fields of inquiry. It is probable that a really fruitful integration of linguistic and psychological studies lies still in the future. We may suspect that linguistics is destined to have a very special value for configurative psychology ('Gestalt psychology'), for, of all forms of culture, it seems that language is that one which develops its fundamental patterns with relatively the most complete detachment from other types of cultural patterning. Linguistics may thus hope to become something of a guide to the understanding of the 'psychological geography' of culture in the large. In ordinary life the basic symbolisms of behavior are densely overlaid by cross-functional patterns of a bewildering variety. It is because every isolated act in human behavior is the meeting point of many distinct configurations that it is so difficult for most of us to arrive at the notion of contextual and non-contextual form in behavior. Linguistics would seem to have a very peculiar value for configurative studies because the patterning of language is to a very appreciable extent self-contained and not significantly at the mercy of inter-crossing patterns of a non-linguistic type.

It is very notable that philosophy in recent years has concerned itself with problems of language as never before. The time is long past when grammatical forms and processes can be naïvely translated by philosophers into metaphysical entities. The philosoopher needs to understand language if only to protect himself against his own language habits, and so it is not surprising that philosophy, in attempting to free logic from the trammels of grammar and to understand knowledge and the meaning of symbolism, is compelled to make a preliminary critique of the linguistic process itself. Linguists should be in an excellent position to assist in the process of making clear to ourselves the implications of our terms and linguistic procedures. Of all students of human behavior, the linguist should by the very nature of his subject matter be the most relativist in feeling, the least taken in by the forms of his own speech.

A word as to the relation between linguistics and the natural sciences. Students of linguistics have been greatly indebted for their technical equipment to the natural sciences, particularly physics and physiology. Phonetics, a necessary prerequisite for all exact work in linguistics, is impossible without some grounding in acoustics and the physiology of the speech organs. It is particularly those students of language who are more interested in the realistic details of actual speech behavior in the individual than in the socialized patterns of language who must have constant recourse to the natural sciences. But it is far from unlikely that the accumulated experience of linguistic research may provide more than one valuable hint for the setting up of problems of research to acoustics and physiology themselves.

All in all, it is clear that the interest in language has in recent years been transcending the strictly linguistic circles. This is inevitable, for an understanding of language mechanisms is necessary for the study of both historical problems and problems of human behavior. One can only hope that linguists will become increasingly aware of the significance of their subject in the general field of science and will not stand aloof behind a tradition that threatens to become scholastic when not vitalized by interests which lie beyond the formal interest in language itself.

Where, finally, does linguistics stand as a science? Does it belong to the natural sciences, with biology, or to the social sciences? There seem to be two facts which are responsible for the persistent tendency to view linguistic data from a biological point of view. In the first place, there is the obvious fact that the actual technique of language behavior involves very specific adjustments of a physiological sort. In the second place, the regularity and typicality of linguistic processes leads to a quasi-romantic feeling of contrast with the apparently free and undetermined behavior of human beings studied from the standpoint of culture. But the regularity of sound change is only superficially analogous to a biological automatism. It is precisely because language is as strictly socialized a type of human behavior as anything else in culture and yet betrays in its outlines and tendencies such regularities as only the natural scientist is in the habit of formulating, that linguistics is of strategic importance for the methodology of social science. Behind the apparent lawlessness of social phenomena there is a regularity of configuration and tendency which is just as real as the regularity of physical processes in a mechanical world, though it is a regularity of infinitely less apparent rigidity and of another mode of apprehension on our part. Language is primarily a cultural or social product and must be understood as such. Its regularity and formal development rest on considerations of a biological and psychological nature, to be sure. But this regularity and our underlying unconsciousness of its typical forms do not make of linguistics a mere adjunct to either biology or psychology. Better than any other social science, linguistics shows by its data and methods, necessarily more easily defined than the data and methods of any other type of discipline dealing with socialized behavior, the possibility of a truly scientific study of society which does not ape the methods nor attempt to adopt unrevised the concepts of the natural sciences. It is peculiarly important that linguists, who are often accused, and accused justly, of failure to look beyond the pretty patterns of their subject matter, should become aware of what their science may mean for the interpretation of human conduct in general. Whether they like it or not, they must become increasingly concerned with the many anthropological, sociological, and psychological problems which invade the field of language.

Culture, Genuine and Spurious

There are certain terms that have a peculiar property. Ostensibly, they mark off specific concepts, concepts that lay claim to a rigorously objective validity. In practice, they label vague terrains of thought that shift or narrow or widen with the point of view of whoso makes use of them, embracing within their gamut of significances conceptions that not only do not harmonize but are in part contradictory. An analysis of such terms soon discloses the fact that underneath the clash of varying contents there is unifying feeling-tone. What makes it possible for so discordant an array of conceptions to answer to the same call is, indeed, precisely this relatively constant halo that surrounds them. Thus, what is "crime" to one man is "nobility" to another, yet both are agreed that crime, whatever it is, is an undesirable category, that nobility, whatever it is, is an estimable one. In the same way, such a term as art may be made to mean divers things, but whatever it means, the term itself demands respectful attention and calls forth, normally, a pleasantly polished state of mind, an expectation of lofty satisfactions. If the particular con-

American Journal of Sociology, vol. 29 (1924), 401–429. Parts of this article were also printed in *The Dalhousie Review*, vol. 2 (1922), 165–178; and in *The Dial*, vol. 67 (1919), 233–236.

ception of art that is advanced or that is implied in a work of art is distasteful to us, we do not express our dissatisfaction by saying, "Then I don't like art." We say this only when we are in a vandalic frame of mind. Ordinarily we get around the difficulty by saying, "But that's not art, it's only pretty-pretty conventionality," or "It's mere sentimentality," or "It's nothing but raw experience, material for art, but not art." We disagree on the value of things and the relations of things, but often enough we agree on the particular value of a label. It is only when the question arises of just where to put the label, that trouble begins. These labels—perhaps we had better call them empty thrones—are enemies of mankind, yet we have no recourse but to make peace with them. We do this by seating our favorite pretenders. The rival pretenders war to the death; the thrones to which they aspire remain serenely splendid in gold.

I desire to advance the claims of a pretender to the throne called "culture." Whatever culture is, we know that it is, or is considered to be, a good thing. I propose to give my idea of what kind of a good thing culture is.

THE VARYING CONCEPTIONS OF CULTURE

The word "culture" seems to be used in three main senses or groups of senses. First of all, culture is technically used by the ethnologist and culture-historian to embody any socially inherited element in the life of man, material and spiritual. Culture so defined is coterminous with man himself, for even the lowliest savages live in a social world characterized by a com-

plex network of traditionally conserved habits, usages, and attitudes. The South African Bushman's
method of hunting game, the belief of the North
American Indian in "medicine," the Periclean Athenian's type of tragic drama, and the electric dynamo
of modern industrialism are all, equally and indifferently, elements of culture, each being an outgrowth
of the collective spiritual effort of man, each being
retained for a given time not as the direct and automatic resultant of purely hereditary qualities but by
means of the more or less consciously imitative
processes summarized by the terms "tradition" and
"social inheritance." From this standpoint all human
beings or, at any rate, all human groups are cultured,
though in vastly different manners and grades of
complexity. For the ethnologist there are many types
of culture and an infinite variety of elements of culture, but no values, in the ordinary sense of the word,
attach to these. His "higher" and "lower," if he uses
the terms at all, refer not to a moral scale of values
but to stages, real or supposed, in a historic progres-
sion or in an evolutionary scheme. I do not intend to
use the term "culture" in this technical sense. "Civilization" would be a convenient substitute for it, were
it not by common usage limited rather to the more
complex and sophisticated forms of the stream of culture. To avoid confusion with other uses of the word
"culture," uses which emphatically involve the application of a scale of values, I shall, where necessary,
use "civilization" in lieu of the ethnologist's "culture."

The second application of the term is more widely
current. It refers to a rather conventional ideal of in-

dividual refinement, built up on a certain modicum of assimilated knowledge and experience but made up chiefly of a set of typical reactions that have the sanction of a class and of a tradition of long standing. Sophistication in the realm of intellectual goods is demanded of the applicant to the title of "cultured person," but only up to a certain point. Far more emphasis is placed upon manner, a certain preciousness of conduct which takes different colors according to the nature of the personality that has assimilated the "cultured" ideal. At its worst, the preciousness degenerates into a scornful aloofness from the manners and tastes of the crowd; this is the well-known cultural snobbishness. At its most subtle, it develops into a mild and whimsical vein of cynicism, an amused skepticism that would not for the world find itself betrayed into an unwonted enthusiasm; this type of cultured manner presents a more engaging countenance to the crowd, which only rarely gets hints of the discomfiting play of its irony, but it is an attitude of perhaps even more radical aloofness than snobbishness outright. Aloofness of some kind is generally a *sine qua non* of the second type of culture. Another of its indispensable requisites is intimate contact with the past. Present action and opinion are, first and foremost, seen in the illumination of a fixed past, a past of infinite richness and glory; only as an afterthought, if at all, are such action and opinion construed as instrumentalities for the building of a future. The ghosts of the past, preferably of the remote past, haunt the cultured man at every step. He is uncannily responsive to their slightest touch; he shrinks from the employment of his individuality as a creative agency. But perhaps the most extraordinary thing about the cultured ideal is its selection of the particular treasures of the past which it deems worthiest of worship. This selection, which might seem bizarre to a mere outsider, is generally justified by a number of reasons, sometimes endowed with a philosophic cast, but unsympathetic persons seem to incline to the view that these reasons are only rationalizations *ad hoc*, that the selection of treasures has proceeded chiefly according to the accidents of history.

In brief, this cultured ideal is a vesture and an air. The vesture may drape gracefully about one's person and the air has often much charm, but the vesture is a ready-made garment for all that and the air remains an air. In America the cultured ideal, in its quintessential classical form, is a more exotic plant than in the halls of Oxford and Cambridge, whence it was imported to these rugged shores, but fragments and derivatives of it meet us frequently enough. The cultured ideal embraces many forms, of which the classical Oxonian form is merely one of the most typical. There are also Chinese and Talmudic parallels. Wherever we find it, it discloses itself to our eyes in the guise of a spiritual heirloom that must, at all cost, be preserved intact.

The third use made of the term is the least easy to define and to illustrate satisfactorily, perhaps because those who use it are so seldom able to give us a perfectly clear idea of just what they themselves mean by culture. Culture in this third sense shares with our first, technical, conception an emphasis on the spiritual possessions of the group rather than of the individual. With our second conception it shares a stressing of selected factors out of the vast whole of the ethnologist's stream of culture as intrinsically more valuable, more characteristic, more significant in a spiritual sense than the rest. To say that this culture embraces all the psychic, as contrasted with the purely material, elements of civilization would not be accurate, partly because the resulting conception would still harbor a vast number of relatively trivial elements, partly because certain of the material factors might well occupy a decisive place in the cultural ensemble. To limit the term, as is sometimes done, to art, religion, and science has again the disadvantage of a too rigid exclusiveness. We may perhaps come nearest the mark by saying that the cultural conception we are now trying to grasp aims to embrace in a single term those general attitudes, views of life, and specific manifestations of civilization that give a particular people its distinctive place in the world. Emphasis is put not so much on what is done and believed by a people as on how what is done and believed functions in the whole life of that people, on what significance it has for them. The very same element of civilization may be a vital strand in the culture of one people, and a well-nigh negligible factor in the culture of another. The present conception of culture is apt to crop up particularly in connection with problems of nationality, with attempts to find embodied in the character and civilization of a given people some peculiar excellence, some distinguishing force, that is strikingly its own. Culture thus becomes nearly synonymous with the "spirit" or "genius" of a people, yet not altogether, for whereas these loosely used terms refer rather to a psychological, or pseudo-psychological, background of national civilization, culture includes with this background a series of concrete manifestations which are believed to be peculiarly symptomatic of it. Culture, then, may be briefly defined as civilization in so far as it embodies the national genius.

Evidently we are on peculiarly dangerous ground here. The current assumption that the so-called "genius" of a people is ultimately reducible to certain inherent hereditary traits of a biological and psychological nature does not, for the most part, bear very serious examination. Frequently enough what is assumed to be an innate racial characteristic turns out on closer study to be the resultant of purely historical causes. A mode of thinking, a distinctive type of reaction, gets itself established, in the course of a complex historical development, as typical, as normal; it serves then as a model for the working over of new elements of civilization. From numerous examples of such distinctive modes of thinking or types of reaction a basic genius is abstracted. There need be no special quarrel with this conception of a national genius so long as it is not worshiped as an irreducible psychological fetish. Ethnologists fight shy of broad generalizations and hazily defined concepts. They are therefore rather timid about operating with national spirits and geniuses. The chauvinism of national apologists, which sees in the spirits of their own peoples peculiar excellences utterly denied to less blessed denizens of the globe, largely justifies this timidity of the scientific students of civilization. Yet here, as so often, the precise knowledge of the scientist lags somewhat behind the more naïve but more powerful insights of nonprofessional experience and impression. To deny to the genius of a people an ultimate psychological significance and to refer it to the specific historical development of that people is not, after all is said and done, to analyze it out of existence. It remains true that large groups of people everywhere tend to think and to act in accordance with established and all but instinctive forms, which are in large measure peculiar to it. The question as to whether these forms, that in their interrelations constitute the genius of a people, are primarily explainable in terms of native temperament, of historical development, or of both is of interest to the social psychologist, but need not cause us much concern. The relevance of this question is not always apparent. It is enough to know that in actual fact nationalities, using the word without political implication, have come to bear the impress in thought and action of a certain mold and that this mold is more clearly discernible in certain elements of civilization than in others. The specific culture of a nationality is that group of elements in its civilization which most emphatically exhibits the mold. In practice it is sometimes convenient to identify the national culture with its genius.

An example or two and we shall have done with

these preliminary definitions. The whole terrain through which we are now struggling is a hotbed of subjectivism, a splendid field for the airing of national conceits. For all that, there are a large number of international agreements in opinion as to the salient cultural characteristics of various peoples. No one who has even superficially concerned himself with French culture can have failed to be impressed by the qualities of clarity, lucid systematization, balance, care in choice of means, and good taste, that permeate so many aspects of the national civilization. These qualities have their weaker side. We are familiar with the overmechanization, the emotional timidity or shallowness (quite a different thing from emotional restraint), the exaggeration of manner at the expense of content, that are revealed in some of the manifestations of the French spirit. Those elements of French civilization that give characteristic evidence of the qualities of its genius may be said, in our present limited sense, to constitute the culture of France; or, to put it somewhat differently, the cultural significance of any element in the civilization of France is in the light it sheds on the French genius. From this standpoint we can evaluate culturally such traits in French civilization as the formalism of the French classical drama, the insistence in French education of the study of the mother-tongue and of its classics, the prevalence of epigram in French life and letters, the intellectualist cast so often given to aesthetic movements in France, the lack of turgidity in modern French music, the relative absence of the ecstatic note in religion, the

strong tendency to bureaucracy in French administration. Each and all of these and hundreds of other
traits could be readily paralleled from the civilization of England. Nevertheless, their relative cultural
significance, I venture to think, is a lesser one in
England than in France. In France they seem to lie
more deeply in the grooves of the cultural mold of
its civilization. Their study would yield something
like a rapid bird's eye view of the spirit of French
culture.

Let us turn to Russia, the culture of which has as
definite a cast as that of France. I shall mention only
one, but that perhaps the most significant, aspect of
Russian culture, as I see it—the tendency of the Russian to see and think of human beings not as repre-
sentatives of types, not as creatures that appear
eternally clothed in the garments of civilization, but
as stark human beings existing primarily in and for
themselves, only secondarily for the sake of civilization. Russian democracy has as its fundamental
aim less the creation of democratic institutions than
the effective liberation of personality itself. The one
thing that the Russian can take seriously is elemental
humanity, and elemental humanity, in his view of
the world, obtrudes itself at every step. He is therefore sublimely at home with himself and his neighbor and with God. Indeed, I have no doubt that
the extremest of Russian atheists is on better speaking terms with God than are the devout of other
lands, to whom God is always something of a mystery. For his environment, including in that term all
the machinery of civilization, the Russian has gen-

erally not a little contempt. The subordination of the
deeps of personality to an institution is not readily
swallowed by him as a necessary price for the blessings of civilization. We can follow out this sweeping
humanity, this almost impertinent prodding of the
real self that lies swathed in civilization, in number-
less forms. In personal relations we may note the
curious readiness of the Russian to ignore all the
institutional barriers which separate man from man;
on its weaker side, this involves at times a personal
irresponsibility that harbors no insincerity. The re-
nunciation of Tolstoi was no isolated phenomenon,
it was a symbol of the deep-seated Russian indifference to institutionalism, to the accreted values of
civilization. In a spiritual sense, it is easy for the
Russian to overthrow any embodiment of the spirit
of institutionalism; his real loyalties are elsewhere.
The Russian preoccupation with elemental humanity
is naturally most in evidence in the realm of art,
where self-expression has freest rein. In the pages of
Tolstoi, Dostoyevski, Turgenev, Gorki, and Chekhov
personality runs riot in its morbid moments of play
with crime, in its depressions and apathies, in its
generous enthusiasms and idealisms. So many of the
figures in Russian literature look out upon life with
a puzzled and incredulous gaze. "This thing that you
call civilization—is that all there is to life?" we hear
them ask a hundred times. In music too the Russian
spirit delights to unmask itself, to revel in the cries
and gestures of man as man. It speaks to us out of
the rugged accents of a Moussorgski as out of the
well-nigh unendurable despair of a Tchaikovski. It

is hard to think of the main current of Russian art as anywhere infected by the dry rot of formalism; we expect some human flash or cry to escape from behind the bars.

I have avoided all attempt to construct a parallel between the spirit of French civilization and that of Russian civilization, between the culture of France and the culture of Russia. Strict parallels force an emphasis on contrasts. I have been content merely to suggest that underlying the elements of civilization, the study of which is the province of the ethnologist and culture-historian is a culture, the adequate interpretation of which is beset with difficulties and which is often left to men of letters.

THE GENUINE CULTURE

The second and third conceptions of the term "culture" are what I wish to make the basis of our genuine culture—the pretender to the throne whose claims to recognition we are to consider. We may accept culture as signifying the characteristic mold of a national civilization, while from the second conception of culture, that of a traditional type of individual refinement, we will borrow the notion of ideal form. Let me say at once that nothing is farther from my mind than to plead the cause of any specific type of culture. It would be idle to praise or blame any fundamental condition of our civilization, to praise or blame any strand in the warp and woof of its genius. These conditions and these strands must be accepted as basic. They are slowly modifiable, to be sure, like everything else in the history of man, but radical modification of fundamentals does not seem necessary for the production of a genuine culture, however much a readjustment of the relations may be. In other words, a genuine culture is perfectly conceivable in any type or stage of civilization, in the mold of any national genius. It can be conceived as easily in terms of a Mohammedan polygamous society, or of an American Indian "primitive" non-agricultural society, as in those of our familiar occidental societies. On the other hand, what may by contrast be called "spurious" cultures are just as easily conceivable in conditions of general enlightenment as in those of relative ignorance and squalor.

The genuine culture is not of necessity either high or low; it is merely inherently harmonious, balanced, self-satisfactory. It is the expression of a richly varied and yet somehow unified and consistent attitude toward life, an attitude which sees the significance of any one element of civilization in its relation to all others. It is, ideally speaking, a culture in which nothing is spiritually meaningless, in which no important part of the general functioning brings with it a sense of frustration, of misdirected or unsympathetic effort. It is not a spiritual hybrid of contradictory patches, of water-tight compartments of consciousness that avoid participation in a harmonious synthesis. If the culture necessitates slavery, it frankly admits it; if it abhors slavery, it feels its way to an economic adjustment that obviates the necessity of its employment. It does not make a great show in its ethical ideals of an uncompromising opposition to slavery, only to introduce what amounts to a slave system into certain portions of its industrial mechanism. Or, if it builds itself magnificent houses of worship, it is because of the necessity it feels to symbolize in beautiful stone a religious impulse that is deep and vital; if it is ready to discard institutionalized religion, it is prepared also to dispense with the homes of institutionalized religion. It does not look sheepish when a direct appeal is made to its religious consciousness, then make amends by furtively donating a few dollars toward the maintenance of an African mission. Nor does it carefully instruct its children in what it knows to be of no use or vitality either to them or in its own mature life. Nor does it tolerate a thousand other spiritual maladjustments such as are patent enough in our American life of today. It would be too much to say that even the purest examples yet known of a genuine culture have been free of spiritual discords, of the dry rot of social habit, devitalized. But the great cultures, those that we instinctively feel to have been healthy spiritual organisms, such as the Athenian culture of the Age of Pericles and, to a less extent perhaps, the English culture of Elizabethan days, have at least tended to such harmony.

It should be clearly understood that this ideal of a genuine culture has no necessary connection with what we call efficiency. A society may be admirably efficient in the sense that all its activities are carefully planned with reference to ends of maximum utility to the society as a whole, it may tolerate no lost motion, yet it may well be an inferior organism as a culture-bearer. It is not enough that the ends of activities be socially satisfactory, that each member of the community feel in some dim way that he is doing his bit toward the attainment of a social benefit. This is all very well so far as it goes, but a genuine culture refuses to consider the individual as a mere cog, as an entity whose sole *raison d'être* lies in his subservience to a collective purpose that he is not conscious of or that has only a remote relevancy to his interests and strivings. The major activities of the individual must directly satisfy his own creative and emotional impulses, must always be something more than means to an end. The great cultural fallacy of industrialism, as developed up to the present time, is that in harnessing machines to our uses it has not known how to avoid the harnessing of the majority of mankind to its machines. The telephone girl who lends her capacities, during the greater part of the living day, to the manipulation of a technical routine that has an eventually high efficiency value but that answers to no spiritual needs of her own is an appalling sacrifice to civilization. As a solution of the problem of culture she is a failure—the more dismal the greater her natural endowment. As with the telephone girl, so, it is to be feared, with the great majority of us, slave-stokers to fires that burn for demons we would destroy, were it not that they appear in the guise of our benefactors. The American Indian who solves the economic problem with salmon-spear and rabbit-snare operates on a relatively low level of civilization, but he represents an incomparably higher solution than our telephone girl of the questions that culture has to ask of economics. There is here no question of the immediate utility, of the effective directness, of economic effort, nor of any sentimentalizing regrets as to the passing of the "natural man." The Indian's salmon-spearing is a culturally higher type of activity than that of the telephone girl or mill hand simply because there is normally no sense of spiritual frustration during its prosecution, no feeling of subservience to tyrannous yet largely inchoate demands, because it works in naturally with all the rest of the Indian's activities instead of standing out as a desert patch of merely economic effort in the whole of life. A genuine culture cannot be defined as a sum of abstractly desirable ends, as a mechanism. It must be looked upon as a sturdy plant growth, each remotest leaf and twig of which is organically fed by the sap at the core. And this growth is not here meant as a metaphor for the group only; it is meant to apply as well to the individual. A culture that does not build itself out of the central interests and desires of its bearers, that works from general ends to the individual, is an external culture. The word "external," which is so often instinctively chosen to describe such a culture, is well chosen. The genuine culture is internal, it works from the individual to ends.

We have already seen that there is no necessary correlation between the development of civilization and the relative genuineness of the culture which forms its spiritual essence. This requires a word of further explanation. By the development of civilization is meant the ever increasing degree of sophis-

tication of our society and of our individual lives.
This progressive sophistication is the inevitable cumulative result of the sifting processes of social experience, of the ever increasing complications of our
innumerable types of organization; most of all of our
steadily growing knowledge of our natural environment and, as a consequence, our practical mastery,
for economic ends, of the resources that nature at
once grants us and hides from us. It is chiefly the
cumulative force of this sophistication that gives us
the sense of what we call "progress." Perched on the
heights of an office building twenty or more stories
taller than our fathers ever dreamed of, we feel that
we are getting up in the world. Hurling our bodies
through space with an ever accelerating velocity, we
feel that we are getting on. Under sophistication I
include not merely intellectual and technical advance, but most of the tendencies that make for a
cleaner and healthier and, to a large extent, a more
humanitarian existence. It is excellent to keep one's
hands spotlessly clean, to eliminate smallpox, to ad-
minister anesthetics. Our growing sophistication, our
ever increasing solicitude to obey the dictates of
common sense, make these tendencies imperative.
It would be sheer obscurantism to wish to stay their
progress. But there can be no stranger illusion—and
it is an illusion we nearly all share—than this, that
because the tools of life are today more specialized
and more refined than ever before, that because the
technique brought by science is more perfect than
anything the world has yet known, it necessarily follows that we are in like degree attaining to a pro-

founder harmony of life, to a deeper and more satisfying culture. It is as though we believed that an elaborate mathematical computation which involved figures of seven and eight digits could not but result in a like figure. Yet we know that one million multiplied by zero gives us zero quite as effectively as one multiplied by zero. The truth is that sophistication, which is what we ordinarily mean by the progress of civilization, is, in the long run, a merely quantitative concept that defines the external conditions for the growth or decay of culture. We are right to have faith in the progress of civilization. We are wrong to assume that the maintenance or even advance of culture is a function of such progress. A reading of the facts of ethnology and culture history proves plainly that maxima of culture have frequently been reached in low levels of sophistication; that minima of culture have been plumbed in some of the highest. Civilization, as a whole, moves on; culture comes and goes.

Every profound change in the flow of civilization, particularly every change in its economic bases, tends to bring about an unsettling and readjustment of cultures values. Old culture forms, habitual types of reaction, tend to persist through the force of inertia. The maladjustment of these habitual reactions to their new civilizational environment brings with it a measure of spiritual disharmony, which the more sensitive individuals feel eventually as a fundamental lack of culture. Sometimes the maladjustment corrects itself with great rapidity, at other times it may persist for generations, as in the case of America, where a chronic state of cultural maladjustment has for so long a period reduced much of our higher life to sterile externality. It is easier, generally speaking, for a genuine culture to subsist on a lower level of civilization; the differentiation of individuals as regards their social and economic functions is so much less than in the higher levels that there is less danger of the reduction of the individual to an unintelligible fragment of the social organism. How to reap the undeniable benefits of a great differentiation of functions, without at the same time losing sight of the individual as a nucleus of live cultural values, is the great and difficult problem of any rapidly complicating civilization. We are far from having solved it in America. Indeed, it may be doubted whether more than an insignificant minority are aware of the existence of the problem. Yet the present world wide labor unrest has as one of its deepest roots some sort of perception of the cultural fallacy of the present form of industrialism.

It is perhaps the sensitive ethnologist who has studied an aboriginal civilization at first hand who is most impressed by the frequent vitality of culture in less sophisticated levels. He cannot but admire the well-rounded life of the average participant in the civilization of a typical American Indian tribe; the firmness with which every part of that life—economic, social, religious, and aesthetic—is bound together into a significant whole in respect to which he is far from a passive pawn; above all, the molding rôle, oftentimes definitely creative, that he plays in the mechanism of his culture. When the political integrity of his tribe is destroyed by contact with the whites and the old cultural values cease to have the atmosphere needed for their continued vitality, the Indian finds himself in a state of bewildered vacuity. Even if he succeeds in making a fairly satisfactory compromise with his new environment, in making what his well-wishers consider great progress toward enlightenment, he is apt to retain an uneasy sense of the loss of some vague and great good, some state of mind that he would be hard put to it to define, but which gave him a courage and joy that latter-day prosperity never quite seems to have regained for him. What has happened is that he has slipped out of the warm embrace of a culture into the cold air of fragmentary existence. What is sad about the passing of the Indian is not the depletion of his numbers by disease nor even the contempt that is too often meted out to him in his life on the reservation, it is the fading away of genuine cultures, built though they were out of the materials of a low order of sophistication.

We have no right to demand of the higher levels of sophistication that they preserve to the individual his manifold functioning, but we may well ask whether, as a compensation, the individual may not reasonably demand an intensification in cultural value, a spiritual heightening, of such functions as are left him. Failing this, he must be admitted to have retrograded. The limitation in functioning works chiefly in the economic sphere. It is therefore imperative, if the individual is to preserve his value as a cultured being, that he compensate himself out of the non-economic, the non-utilitarian spheres—social, religious, scientific, aesthetic. This idea of compensation brings to view an important issue, that of the immediate and the remoter ends of human effort.

As a mere organism, man's only function is to exist; in other words, to keep himself alive and to propagate his kind. Hence the procuring of food, clothing, and shelter for himself and those dependent on him constitutes the immediate end of his effort. There are civilizations, like that of the Eskimo, in which by far the greater part of man's energy is consumed in the satisfaction of these immediate ends, in which most of his activities contribute directly or indirectly to the procuring and preparation of food and the materials for clothing and shelter. There are practically no civilizations, however, in which at least some of the available energy is not set free for the remoter ends, though, as a rule, these remoter ends are by a process of rationalization made to seem to contribute to the immediate ones. (A magical ritual, for instance, which, when considered psychologically, seems to liberate and give form to powerful emotional aesthetic elements of our nature, is nearly always put in harness to some humdrum utilitarian end—the catching of rabbits or the curing of disease.) As a matter of fact, there are very few "primitive" civilizations that do not consume an exceedingly large share of their energies in the pursuit of the remoter ends, though it remains true that these remoter ends are nearly always functionally or pseudo-functionally interwoven with the immediate ends. Art for art's sake may be a psychological fact on these less sophisticated levels; it is certainly not a cultural fact.

On our own level of civilization the remoter ends tend to split off altogether from the immediate ones and to assume the form of a spiritual escape or refuge from the pursuit of the latter. The separation of the two classes of ends is never absolute nor can it ever be; it is enough to note the presence of a powerful drift of the two away from each other. It is easy to demonstrate this drift by examples taken out of our daily experience. While in most primitive civilizations the dance is apt to be a ritual activity at least ostensibly associated with purposes of an economic nature, it is with us a merely and self-consciously pleasurable activity that not only splits off from the sphere of the pursuit of immediate ends but even tends to assume a position of hostility to that sphere. In a primitive civilization a great chief dances as a matter of course, oftentimes as a matter of exercising a peculiarly honored privilege. With us the captain of industry either refuses to dance at all or does so as a half-contemptuous concession to the tyranny of social custom. On the other hand, the artist of a Ballet Russe has sublimated the dance to an exquisite instrument of self-expression, has succeeded in providing himself with an adequate, or more than adequate, cultural recompense for his loss of mastery in the realm of direct ends. The captain of industry is one of the comparatively small class of individuals that has inherited, in vastly complicated form, something of the feeling of control over the attainment of direct ends that belongs by cultural right to primitive man; the ballet dancer has saved and intensified for himself the feeling of spontaneous participation and creativeness in the world of indirect ends that also belongs by cultural right to primitive man. Each has saved part of the wreckage of a submerged culture for himself.

The psychology of direct and indirect ends undergoes a gradual modification, only partly consummated as yet, in the higher levels of civilization. The immediate ends continue to exercise the same tyrannical sway in the ordering of our lives, but as our spiritual selves become enriched and develop a more and more inordinate craving for subtler forms of experience, there develops also an attitude of impatience with the solution of the more immediate problems of life. In other words, the immediate ends cease to be felt as chief ends and gradually become necessary means, but only means, toward the attainment of the more remote ends. These remoter ends, in turn, so far from being looked upon as purely incidental activities which result from the spilling over of an energy concentrated almost entirely on the pursuit of the immediate ends, become the chief ends of life. This change of attitude is implied in the statement that the art, science, and religion of a higher civilization best express its spirit or culture. The transformation of ends thus briefly outlined is far from an accomplished fact; it is rather an obscure drift in the history of values, an expression of the volition of the more sensitive participants in our culture. Certain temperaments feel themselves impelled far along the drift, others lag behind.

The transformation of ends is of the greatest cultural importance because it acts as a powerful force for the preservation of culture in levels in which a fragmentary economic functioning of the individual is inevitable. So long as the individual retains a sense of control over the major goods of life, he is able to take his place in the cultural patrimony of his people. Now that the major goods of life have shifted so largely from the realm of immediate to that of remote ends, it becomes a cultural necessity for all who would not be looked upon as disinherited to share in the pursuit of these remoter ends. No harmony and depth of life, no culture, is possible when activity is well-nigh circumscribed by the sphere of immediate ends and when functioning within that sphere is so fragmentary as to have no inherent intelligibility or interest. Here lies the grimmest joke of our present American civilization. The vast majority of us, deprived of any but an insignificant and culturally abortive share in the satisfaction of the immediate wants of mankind, are further deprived of both opportunity and stimulation to share in the production of non-utilitarian values. Part of the time we are dray horses; the rest of the time we are listless consumers of goods which have received no least impress of our personality. In other words, our spiritual selves go hungry, for the most part, pretty much all of the time.

THE CULTURED INDIVIDUAL
AND THE CULTURAL GROUP

There is no real opposition, at last analysis, between

the concept of a culture of the group and the concept of an individual culture. The two are interdependent. A healthy national culture is never a passively accepted heritage from the past, but implies the creative participation of the members of the community; implies, in other words, the presence of cultured individuals. An automatic perpetuation of standardized values, not subject to the constant remodeling of individuals willing to put some part of themselves into the forms they receive from their predecessors, leads to the dominance of impersonal formulas. The individual is left out in the cold; the culture becomes a manner rather than a way of life, it ceases to be genuine. It is just as true, however, that the individual is helpless without a cultural heritage to work on. He cannot, out of his unaided spiritual powers, weave a strong cultural fabric instinct with the flush of his own personality. Creation is a bending of form to one's will, not a manufacture of form *ex nihilo*. If the passive perpetuator of a cultural tradition gives us merely a manner, the shell of a life that once was, the creator from out of a cultural waste gives us hardly more than a gesture or a yawp, the strident promise of a vision raised by our desires.

There is a curious notion afloat that "new" countries are especially favorable soil for the formation of a virile culture. By new is meant something old that has been transplanted to a background devoid of historical associations. It would be remarkable if a plant, flourishing in heavy black loam, suddenly acquired a new virility on transplantation into a shallow sandy soil. Metaphors are dangerous things that prove nothing, but experience suggests the soundness of this particular metaphor. Indeed, there is nothing more tenuous, more shamelessly imitative and external, less virile and self-joyous, than the cultures of so-called "new countries." The environments of these transplanted cultures are new, the cultures themselves are old with the sickly age of arrested development. If signs of a genuine blossoming of culture are belatedly beginning to appear in America, it is not because America is still new; rather is America coming of age, beginning to feel a little old. In a genuinely new country, the preoccupation with the immediate ends of existence reduces creativeness in the sphere of the more remote ends to a minimum. The net result is a perceptible dwarfing of culture. The old stock of non-material cultural goods lingers on without being subjected to vital remodelings, becomes progressively impoverished, and ends by being so hopelessly ill adjusted to the economic and social environment that the more sensitive spirits tend to break with it altogether and to begin anew with a frank recognition of the new environmental conditions. Such new starts are invariably crude; they are long in bearing the fruits of a genuine culture.

It is only an apparent paradox that the subtlest and the most decisive cultural influences of personality, the most fruitful revolts, are discernible in those environments that have long and uninterruptedly supported a richly streaming culture. So far from being suffocated in an atmosphere of endless precedent, the creative spirit gains sustenance and vigor for its own unfolding and, if it is strong enough, it may swing free of that very atmosphere with a poise hardly dreamed of by the timid iconoclasts of unformed cultures. Not otherwise could we understand the cultural history of modern Europe. Only in a mature and richly differentiated soil could arise the iconoclasms and visions of an Anatole France, a Nietzsche, an Ibsen, a Tolstoi. In America, at least in the America of yesterday, these iconoclasms and these visions would either have been strangled in the cradle, or, had they found air to breathe, they would have half-developed into a crude and pathetic isolation. There is no sound and vigorous individual incorporation of a cultured ideal without the soil of a genuine communal culture; and no genuine communal culture without the transforming energies of personalities at once robust and saturated with the cultural values of their time and place. The highest type of culture is thus locked in the embrace of an endless chain, to the forging of which goes much labor, weary and protracted. Such a culture avoids the two extremes of "externality"— the externality of surfeit, which weighs down the individual, and the externality of barrenness. The former is the decay of Alexandrianism, in which the individual is no more; the latter, the combined immaturity and decay of an uprooted culture, in which the individual is not yet. Both types of externality may be combined in the same culture, frequently in the same person. Thus, it is not uncommon to find in America individuals who have had engrafted on a

barren and purely utilitarian culture a cultural tradition that apes a grace already embalmed. One
surmises that this juxtaposition of incongruous at-
mospheres is even typical in certain circles.

Let us look a little more closely at the place of the
individual in a modern sophisticated culture. I have
insisted throughout that a genuine culture is one that
gives its bearers a sense of inner satisfaction, a feeling of spiritual mastery. In the higher levels of civilization this sense of mastery is all but withdrawn,
as we have seen, from the economic sphere. It must,
then, to an even greater extent than in more primitive civilizations, feed on the non-economic spheres
of human activity. The individual is thus driven, or
should be if he would be truly cultured, to the identification of himself with some portion of the wide
range of non-economic interests. From the standpoint adopted in this study, this does not mean that
the identification is a purely casual and acquisitive
process; it is, indeed, made not so much for its own
sake as in order to give the self the wherewithal to
develop its powers. Concretely considered, this
would mean, for instance, that a mediocre person
moderately gifted with the ability to express his
aesthetic instincts in plastic form and exercising the
gift in his own sincere and humble way (to the neglect, it may be, of practically all other interests) is
ipso facto a more cultured individual than a person
of brilliant endowments who has acquainted himself in a general way with all the "best" that has
been thought and felt and done, but who has never
succeeded in bringing any portion of his range of

interests into direct relation with his volitional self, with the innermost shrine of his personality. An individual of the latter type, for all his brilliance, we call "flat." A flat person cannot be truly cultured. He may, of course, be highly cultured in the conventional sense of the word "culture," but that is another story. I would not be understood as claiming that direct creativeness is essential, though it is highly desirable, for the development of individual culture. To a large extent it is possible to gain a sense of the required mastery by linking one's own personality with that of the great minds and hearts that society has recognized as its significant creators. Possible, that is, so long as such linking, such vicarious experience, is attended by some portion of the effort, the fluttering toward realization that is inseparable from all creative effort. It is to be feared, however, that the self-discipline that is here implied is none too often practiced. The linking, as I have called it, of self with master soul too often degenerates into a pleasurable servitude, into a facile abnegation of one's own individuality, the more insidious that it has the approval of current judgment. The pleasurable servitude may degenerate still further into a vice. Those of us who are not altogether blind can see in certain of our acquaintances, if not in ourselves, an indulgence in aesthetic or scientific goods that is strictly comparable to the abuse of alcoholic intoxicants. Both types of self-ignoring or self-submerging habit are signs of a debilitated personality; both are antithetical to the formation of culture.

The individual self, then, in aspiring to culture,

fastens upon the accumulated cultural goods of its
society, not so much for the sake of the passive
pleasure of their acquirement, as for the sake of the
stimulus given to the unfolding personality and of
the orientation derived in the world (or better, a
world) of cultural values. The orientation, conventional as it may be, is necessary if only to give the
self a *modus vivendi* with society at large. The individual needs to assimilate much of the cultural
background of his society, many of the current sentiments of his people, to prevent his self-expression
from degenerating into social sterility. A spiritual
hermit may be genuinely cultured, but he is hardly
socially so. To say that individual culture must needs
grow organically out of the rich soil of a communal
culture is far from saying that it must be forever tied
to that culture by the leading strings of its own
childhood. Once the individual self has grown strong
enough to travel in the path most clearly illuminated
by its own light, it not only can but should discard
much of the scaffolding by which it has made its
ascent. Nothing is more pathetic than the persistence
with which well-meaning applicants to culture attempt to keep up or revive cultural stimuli which
have long outlived their significance for the growth
of personality. To keep up or brush up one's Greek,
for example, in those numerous cases in which a
knowledge of Greek has ceased to bear a genuine
relation to the needs of the spirit, is almost a spiritual crime. It is acting "the dog in the manger" with
one's own soul. If the traveling in the path of the
self's illumination leads to a position that is destruc-

tive of the very values the self was fed on, as happened, though in very different ways, with Nietzsche and with Tolstoi, it has not in the slightest lost touch with genuine culture. It may well, on the contrary, have arrived at its own highest possible point of culture development.

Nietzsche and Tolstoi, however, are extreme types of personality. There is no danger that the vast army of cultured humanity will ever come to occupy spiritual positions of such rigor and originality. The real danger, as is so abundantly attested by daily experience, is in submitting to the remorselessly leveling forces of a common cultural heritage and of the action of average mind on average mind. These forces will always tend to a general standardization of both the content and the spirit of culture, so powerfully, indeed, that the centrifugal effect of robust, self-sustaining personalities need not be feared. The caution to conformity with tradition, which the champions of culture so often feel themselves called upon to announce, is one that we can generally dispense with. It is rather the opposite caution, the caution to conformity with the essential nature of one's own personality, that needs urging. It needs to be urged as a possible counter-irritant to the flat and tedious sameness of spiritual outlook, the anemic make-believe, the smug intolerance of the challenging, that so imprison our American souls.

No greater test of the genuineness of both individual and communal culture can be applied than the attitude adopted toward the past, its institutions, its treasures of art and thought. The genuinely cultured individual or society does not contemptuously reject the past. They honor the works of the past, but not because they are gems of historical chance, not because, being out of our reach, they must needs be looked at through the enshrining glass of museum cases. These works of the past still excite our heartfelt interest and sympathy because, and only in so far as, they may be recognized as the expression of a human spirit warmly akin, despite all differences of outward garb, to our own. This is very nearly equivalent to saying that the past is of cultural interest only when it is still the present or may yet become the future. Paradoxical as it may seem, the historical spirit has always been something of an anticultural force, has always acted in some measure as an unwitting deterrent of the cultural utilization of the past. The historical spirit says, "Beware, those thoughts and those feelings that you so rashly think to embody in the warp and woof of your own spirit—they are of other time and of other place and they issue from alien motives. In bending over them you do but obscure them with the shadow of your own spirit." This cool reserve is an excellent mood for the making of historical science; its usefulness to the building of culture in the present is doubtful. We know immensely more about Hellenic antiquity in these days than did the scholars and artists of the Renaissance; it would be folly to pretend that our live utilization of the Hellenic spirit, accurately as we merely know it, is comparable to the inspiration, the creative stimulus, that those men of the Renaissance obtained from its fragmentary and garbled tradition. It is difficult to think of a renaissance of that type as thriving in the critical atmosphere of today. We should walk so gingerly in the paths of the past for fear of stepping on anachronisms, that, wearied with fatigue, we should finally sink into a heavy doze, to be awakened only by the insistent clatter of the present. It may be that in our present state of sophistication such a spirit of criticism, of detachment, is not only unavoidable but essential for the preservation of our own individualities. The past is now more of a past than ever before. Perhaps we should expect less of it than ever before. Or rather expect no more of it than it hold its portals wide open, that we may enter in and despoil it of what bits we choose for our pretty mosaics. Can it be that the critical sense of history, which galvanizes the past into scientific life, is destined to slay it for the life of culture? More probably, what is happening is that the spiritual currents of today are running so fast, so turbulently, that we find it difficult to get a culturally vital perspective of the past, which is thus, for the time being, left as a glorified mummy in the hands of the pundits. And, for the time being, those others of us who take their culture neither as knowledge nor as manner, but as life, will ask of the past not so much "what?" and "when?" and "where?" as "how?" and the accent of their "how" will be modulated in accordance with the needs of the spirit of each, a spirit that is free to glorify, to transform, and to reject.

To summarize the place of the individual in our theory of culture, we may say that the pursuit of genuine culture implies two types of reconciliation. The self seeks instinctively for mastery. In the process of acquiring a sense of mastery that is not crude but proportioned to the degree of sophistication proper to our time, the self is compelled to suffer an abridgment and to undergo a molding. The extreme differentiation of function which the progress of man has forced upon the individual menaces the spirit; we have no recourse but to submit with good grace to this abridgment of our activity, but it must not be allowed to clip the wings of the spirit unduly. This is the first and most important reconciliation—the finding of a full world of spiritual satisfactions within the straight limits of an unwontedly confined economic activity. The self must set itself at a point where it can, if not embrace the whole spiritual life of its group, at least catch enough of its rays to burst into light and flame. Moreover, the self must learn to reconcile its own strivings, its own imperious necessities, with the general spiritual life of the community. It must be content to borrow sustenance from the spiritual consciousness of that community and of its past, not merely that it may obtain the wherewithal to grow at all, but that it may grow where its power, great or little, will be brought to bear on a spiritual life that is of intimate concern to other wills. Yet, despite all reconciliations, the self has a right to feel that it grows as an integral, self-poised, spiritual growth, whose ultimate justifications rest in itself, whose sacrifices and compensations must be justified to itself. The conception of the self as a mere instrument toward the attainment of communal ends, whether of state or other social body, is to be discarded as leading in the long run to psychological absurdities and to spiritual slavery. It is the self that concedes, if there is to be any concession. Spiritual freedom, what there is of it, is not alms dispensed, now indifferently, now grudgingly, by the social body. That a different philosophy of the relation of the individual to his group is now so prevalent, makes it all the more necessary to insist on the spiritual primacy of the individual soul.

It is a noteworthy fact that wherever there is discussion of culture, emphasis is instinctively placed upon art. This applies as well to individual as to communal culture. We apply the term "cultured" only with reserve to an individual in whose life the aesthetic moment plays no part. So also, if we would catch something of the spirit, the genius, of a bygone period or of an exotic civilization, we turn first and foremost to its art. A thoughtless analysis would see in this nothing but the emphasis on the beautiful, the decorative, that comports with the conventional conception of culture as a life of traditionally molded refinement. A more penetrating analysis discards such an interpretation. For it the highest manifestations of culture, the very quintessence of the genius of a civilization, necessarily rest in art, for the reason that art is the authentic expression, in satisfying form, of experience; experience not as logically ordered by science, but as directly and intuitively presented to us in life. As culture rests, in essence, on the harmonious development of the sense of mastery instinctively sought by each individual soul, this can only mean that art, the form of consciousness in which the impress of the self is most direct, least hampered by outward necessity, is above all other undertakings of the human spirit bound to reflect culture. To relate *our* lives, *our* intuitions, *our* passing moods to forms of expression that carry conviction to others and make us live again in these others is the highest spiritual satisfaction we know of, the highest welding of one's individuality with the spirit of his civilization. Were art ever really perfect in expression, it would indeed be immortal. Even the greatest art, however, is full of the dross of conventionality, of the particular sophistications of its age. As these change, the directness of expression in any work of art tends to be increasingly felt as hampered by a something fixed and alien, until it gradually falls into oblivion. While art lives, it belongs to culture; in the degree that it takes on the frigidity of death, it becomes of interest only to the study of civilization. Thus all art appreciation (and production, for that matter) has two faces. It is unfortunate that the face directed to civilization is so often confounded with that which is fixed on culture.

THE GEOGRAPHY OF CULTURE

An oft-noted peculiarity of the development of culture is the fact that it reaches its greatest heights in comparatively small, autonomous groups. In fact, it is doubtful if a genuine culture ever properly belongs to more than such a restricted group, a group between the members of which there can be said to be something like direct intensive spiritual contact. This direct contact is enriched by the common cultural heritage on which the minds of all are fed; it is rendered swift and pregnant by the thousands of feelings and ideas that are tacitly assumed and that constantly glimmer in the background. Such small, culturally autonomous groups were the Athens of the Periclean Age, the Rome of Augustus, the independent city-states of Italy in late medieval times, the London of Elizabethan days, and the Paris of the last three centuries. It is customary to speak of certain of these groups and of their cultures as though they were identical with, or represented, widely extended groups and cultures. To a curiously large extent such usages are really figures of speech, substitutions of a part for the whole. It is astonishing, for instance, how much the so-called "history of French literature" is really the history of literary activity in the city of Paris. True enough, a narrowly localized culture may, and often does, spread its influence far beyond its properly restricted sphere. Sometimes it sets the pace for a whole nationality, for a far-flung empire. It can do so, however, only at the expense of diluting in spirit as it moves away from its home, of degenerating into an imitative attitudinizing. If we realized more keenly what the rapid spread or imposition of a culture entails, to what an extent it conquers by crushing the germs of healthier autonomous growths, we would be less eager to welcome uniformizing tendencies, less ready to think of them as progressive in character. A culture may well be quickened from without, but its supersession by another, whether superior or not, is no cultural gain. Whether or not it is attended by a political gain does not concern us here. That is why the deliberate attempt to impose a culture directly and speedily, no matter how backed by good will, is an affront to the human spirit. When such an attempt is backed, not by good will, but by military ruthlessness, it is the greatest conceivable crime against the human spirit, it is the very denial of culture.

Does this mean that we must turn our back on all internationalistic tendencies and vegetate forever in our nationalisms? Here we are confronted by the prevalent fallacy that internationalism is in spirit opposed to the intensive development of autonomous cultures. The fallacy proceeds from a failure to realize that internationalism, nationalism, and localism are forms that can be given various contents. We cannot intelligently discuss internationalism before we know what it is that we are to be internationalistic about. Unfortunately we are so obsessed by the idea of subordinating all forms of human association to the state and of regarding the range of all types of activity as conterminous with political boundaries, that it is difficult for us to reconcile the idea of a local or restrictedly national autonomy of culture with a purely political state-sovereignty and with an economic-political internationalism.

No one can see clearly what is destined to be the larger outcome of the present world conflicts. They may exacerbate rather than allay national-political animosities and thus tend to strengthen the prestige of the state. But this deplorable result cannot well be other than a passing phase. Even now it is evident that the war has, in more ways than one, paved the way for an economic and, as a corollary, a semi-political internationalism. All those spheres of activity that relate to the satisfaction of immediate ends, which, from the vantage point that we have gained, are nothing but means, will tend to become international functions. However the internationalizing processes will shape themselves in detail, they will at bottom be but the reflection of that growing impatience of the human spirit with the preoccupation with direct ends, which I spoke of before. Such transnational problems as the distribution of economic goods, the transportation of commodities, the control of highways, the coinage, and numerous others, must eventually pass into the hands of international organizations for the simple reason that men will not eternally give their loyalty to the uselessly national administration of functions that are of inherently international scope. As this international scope gets to be thoroughly realized, our present infatuations with national prestige in the economic sphere will show themselves for the spiritual imbecilities that they are.

All this has much to do with the eventual development of culture. As long as culture is looked upon as a decorative appanage of large political units, one can plausibly argue that its preservation is bound up with the maintenance of the prestige of these units. But genuine culture is inconceivable except on the basis of a highly individual spiritual consciousness, it rarely remains healthy and subtle when spread thin over an interminable area, and in its higher reaches it is in no mood to submit to economic and political bonds. Now a generalized international culture is hardly thinkable. The national-political unit tends to arrogate culture to itself and up to a certain point it succeeds in doing so, but only at the price of serious cultural impoverishment of vast portions of its terrain. If the economic and political integrity of these large state-controlled units becomes gradually undermined by the growth of international functions, their cultural *raison d'être* must also tend to weaken. Culture must then tend with ever increasing intensity to cling to relatively small social and to minor political units, units that are not too large to incorporate the individuality that is to culture as the very breath of life. Between these two processes, the integration of economic and political forces into a world sovereignty and the disintegration of our present unwieldy culture units into small units whose life is truly virile and individual, the fetish of the present state, with its uncontrolled sovereignty, may in the dim future be trusted to melt away. The political state of today has long been on trial and has been found wanting. Our national-political units are too small for peace, too large for safety. They are too small for the intelligent solution of the large problems in the sphere of direct ends; they are too large for the fruitful enrichment of the remoter ends, for culture.

It is in the New World, perhaps more than in any other part of the globe, that the unsatisfactory nature of a geographically widespread culture, of little depth or individuality to begin with, is manifest. To find substantially the same cultural manifestions, material

and spiritual, often indeed to the minutest details, in
New York and Chicago and San Francisco is sadden-
ing. It argues a shallowness in the culture itself and a
readiness to imitation in its bearers that is not reassuring. Even if no definite way out of the flat cultural
morass is clearly discernible for the present, there is
no good in basking forever in self-sufficiency. It can
only be of benefit to search out the depths of our
hearts and to find wherein they are wanting. If we
exaggerate our weakness, it does not matter; better
chastening than self-glorification. We have been in
the habit of giving ourselves credit for essentially
quantitative results that are due rather to an unusu-
ally favoring nature and to a favoring set of economic conditions than to anything in ourselves. Our
victories have been brilliant, but they have also too
often been barren for culture. The habit of playing
with loaded dice has given us a dangerous attitude
of passivity—dangerous, that is, for culture. Stretching back opulently in our easy chairs, we expect
great cultural things to happen to us. We have
wound up the machinery, and admirable machinery
it is; it is "up to" culture to come forth, in heavy pan-
oply. The minute increment of individuality which
alone makes culture in the self and eventually builds
up a culture in the community seems somehow overlooked. Canned culture is so much easier to adminis-
ter.

Just now we are expecting a great deal from the
European war. No doubt the war and its aftermath
will shake us out of some part of our smugness and
let in a few invigorating air currents of cultural in-

fluence, but, if we are not careful, these influences may soon harden into new standardizations or become diluted into another stock of imitative attitudes and reactions. The war and its aftermath cannot be a sufficient cultural cause, they are at best but another set of favoring conditions. We need not be too much astonished if a Periclean culture does not somehow automatically burst into bloom. Sooner or later we shall have to get down to the humble task of exploring the depths of our consciousness and dragging to the light what sincere bits of reflected experience we can find. These bits will not always be beautiful, they will not always be pleasing, but they will be genuine. And then we can build. In time, in plenty of time—for we must have patience—a genuine culture—better yet, a series of linked autonomous cultures—will grace our lives. And New York and Chicago and San Francisco will live each in its own cultural strength, not squinting from one to another to see which gets ahead in a race for external values, but each serenely oblivious of its rivals because growing in a soil of genuine cultural values.

The Meaning of Religion

A very useful distinction can be made between "a religion" and "religion." The former appears only in a highly developed society in which religious behavior has been organized by tradition; the latter is universal.

The ordinary conception of a religion includes the notions of a self-conscious "church," of religious officers whose functions are clearly defined by custom and who typically engage in no other type of economic activity, and of carefully guarded rituals which are the symbolic expression of the life of the church. Generally, too, such a religion is invested with a certain authority by a canonical tradition which has grown up around a body of sacred texts, supposed to have been revealed by God or to have been faithfully set down by the founder of the religion or by followers of His who have heard the sacred words from His own lips.

If we leave the more sophisticated peoples and study the social habits of primitive and barbaric folk, we shall find that it is very difficult to discover religious institutions that are as highly formalized as

The American Mercury, vol. 15 (September, 1928), 72–79. Published also under the title "Religions and Religious Phenomena," in Baker Brownell, ed., *Religious Life* (New York, D. Van Nostrand Company, 1929), pp. 11–33.

those that go under the name of the Roman Catholic Church or of Judaism. Yet religion in some sense is everywhere present. It seems to be as universal as speech itself and the use of material tools. It is difficult to apply a single one of the criteria which are ordinarily used to define a religion to the religious behavior of primitive peoples, yet neither the absence of specific religious officers nor the lack of authoritative religious texts nor any other conventional lack can seriously mislead the student into denying them true religion. Ethnologists are unanimous in ascribing religious behavior to the very simplest of known societies. So much of a commonplace, indeed, is this assumption of the presence of religion in every known community—barring none, not even those that flaunt the banner of atheism—that one needs to reaffirm and justify the assumption.

How are we to define religion? Can we get behind priests and prayers and gods and rituals and discover a formula that is not too broad to be meaningless nor so specific as to raise futile questions of exclusion or inclusion? I believe it is possible to do this if we ignore for a moment the special forms of behavior deemed religious and attend to the essential meaning and function of such behavior. Religion is precisely one of those words that belong to the more intuitive portion of our vocabulary. We can often apply it safely and unexpectedly without the slightest concern for whether the individual or group termed religious is priest-ridden or not, is addicted to prayer or not, or believes or does not believe in a god. Almost unconsciously the term has come to have for most of us a certain connotation of personality. Some individuals are religious and others are not, and all societies have religion in the sense that they provide the naturally religious person with certain ready-made symbols for the exercise of his religious need.

The formula that I would venture to suggest is simply this: Religion is man's never-ceasing attempt to discover a road to spiritual serenity across the perplexities and dangers of daily life. How this serenity is obtained is a matter of infinitely varied detail. Where the need for such serenity is passionately felt, we have religious yearning; where it is absent, religious behavior is no more than socially sanctioned form or an æsthetic blend of belief and gesture. In practice it is all but impossible to disconnect religious sentiment from formal religious conduct, but it is worth divorcing the two in order that we may insist all the more clearly on the reality of the sentiment.

What constitutes spiritual serenity must be answered afresh for every culture and for every community—in the last analysis, for every individual. Culture defines for every society the world in which it lives, hence we can expect no more of any religion than that it awaken and overcome the feeling of danger, of individual helplessness, that is proper to that particular world. The ultimate problems of an Ojibwa Indian are different as to content from those of the educated devotee of modern science, but with each of them religion means the haunting realization of ultimate powerlessness in an inscrutable world, and the unquestioning and thoroughly irrational conviction of the possibility of gaining mystic security by somehow identifying oneself with what can never be known. Religion is omnipresent fear and a vast humility paradoxically turned into bedrock security, for once the fear is imaginatively taken to one's heart and the humility confessed for good and all, the triumph of human consciousness is assured. There can be neither fear nor humiliation for deeply religious natures, for they have intuitively experienced both of these emotions in advance of the declared hostility of an overwhelming world, coldly indifferent to human desire.

Religion of such purity as I have defined it is hard to discover. That does not matter; it is the pursuit, conscious or unconscious, of ultimate serenity following total and necessary defeat that constitutes the core of religion. It has often allied itself with art and science, and art at least has gained from the alliance, but in crucial situations religion has always shown itself indifferent to both. Religion seeks neither the objective enlightenment of science nor the strange equilibrium, the sensuous harmony, of æsthetic experience. It aims at nothing more nor less than the impulsive conquest of reality, and it can use science and art as little more than stepping stones toward the attainment of its own serenity. The mind that is intellectualist through and through is necessarily baffled by religion, and in the attempt to explain it makes little more of it than a blind and chaotic science.

Whether or not the spirit of religion is reconcilable with that of art does not concern us. Human nature

is infinitely complex and every type of reconciliation of opposites seems possible, but it must be insisted that the nucleus of religious feeling is by no
means identical with æsthetic emotion. The serenity
of art seems of an utterly different nature from that
of religion. Art creates a feeling of wholeness precipi-
tating the flux of things into tangible forms, beautiful
and sufficient to themselves; religion gathers up all
the threads and meaninglessnesses of life into a
wholeness that is not manifest and can only be experienced in the form of a passionate desire. It is not
useful and it is perhaps not wise to insist on fundamental antinomies, but if one were pressed to the
wall one might perhaps be far from wrong in suspect-
ing that the religious spirit is antithetical to that of
art, for religion is essentially ultimate and irreconcilable. Art forgives because it values as an ultimate
good the here and now; religion forgives because the
here and now are somehow irrelevant to a desire that
drives for ultimate solutions.

II

Religion does not presuppose a definite belief in God
or in a number of gods or spirits, though in practice
such beliefs are generally the rationalized background for religious behavior.

Belief, as a matter of fact, is not a properly religious concept at all, but a scientific one. The sum
total of one's beliefs may be said to constitute one's
science. Some of these beliefs can be sustained by
an appeal to direct personal experience, others rest

for their warrant on the authority of society or on the authority of such individuals as are known or believed to hold in their hands the keys of final demonstration. So far as the normal individual is concerned, a belief in the reality of molecules or atoms is of exactly the same nature as a belief in God or immortality. The true division here is not between science and religious belief, but between personally verifiable and personally unverifiable belief. A philosophy of life is not religion if the phrase connotes merely a cluster of rationalized beliefs. Only when one's philosophy of life is vitalized by emotion does it take on the character of religion.

Some writers have spoken of a specifically religious emotion, but it seems quite unnecessary to appeal to any such hypothetical concept. One may rest content to see in religious emotion nothing more nor less than a cluster of such typical emotional experiences as fear, awe, hope, love, the pleading attitude, and any others that may be experienced, in so far as these psychological experiences occur in a context of ultimate values. Fear as such, no matter how poignant or ecstatic, is not religion. A calm belief in a God who creates and rewards and punishes does not constitute religion if the believer fails to recognize the necessity of the application of this belief to his personal problems. Only when the emotion of fear and the belief in a God are somehow integrated into a value can either the emotion or the belief be said to be of a religious nature. This standpoint allows for no specific religious emotions nor does it recognize any specific forms of belief as necessary for religion.

All that is asked is that intensity of feeling join with a philosophy of ultimate things into an unanalyzed conviction of the possibility of security in a world of values.

One can distinguish, in theory if not in practice, between individual religious experience and socialized religious behavior. Some writers on religion put the emphasis on the reality and intensity of the individual experience, others prefer to see in religion a purely social pattern, an institution on which the individual must draw in order to have religious experience at all. The contrast between these two points of view is probably more apparent than real. The suggestions for religious behavior will always be found to be of social origin; it is the validation of this behavior in individual or in social terms that may be thought to vary. This is equivalent to saying that some societies tend to seek the most intense expression of religious experience in individual behavior (including introspection under that term), while others tend toward a collective orthodoxy, reaching an equivalent intensity of life in forms of behavior in which the individual is subordinated to a collective symbol. Religions that conform to the first tendency may be called evangelistic, and those of the second type ritualistic.

The contrast invites criticism, as everyone who has handled religious data knows. One may object that it is precisely under the stimulation of collective activity, as in the sun dance of the Plains Indians or in the Roman Catholic mass, that the most intense forms of individual experience are created. Again, one may see in the most lonely and self-centered of religious practices, say the mystic ecstasies of a saint or the private prayer of one lost to society, little more than the religious behavior of society itself, disconnected, for the moment, from the visible church. A theorist like Durkheim sees the church implicit in every prayer or act of ascetic piety. It is doubtful if the mere observation of religious behavior quite justifies the distinction that I have made. A finer psychological analysis would probably show that the distinction is none the less valid—that societies differ or tend to differ according to whether they find the last court of appeal in matters religious, in the social act, or in the private emotional experience.

Let one example do for many. The religion of the Plains Indians is different in many of its details from that of the Pueblo Indians of the Southwest. Nevertheless there are many external resemblances between them, such as the use of shrines with fetishistic objects gathered in them, the color symbolism of cardinal points, and the religious efficacy of communal dancing. It is not these and a host of other resemblances, however, that impress the student of native American religion; it is rather their profound psychological difference. The Plains Indians' religion is full of collective symbols; indeed, a typical ethnological account of the religion of a Plains tribe seems to be little more than a list of social stereotypes—dances and regalia and taboos and conventional religious tokens. The sun dance is an exceedingly elaborate ritual which lasts many days and in which each song and each step in the progress of the ceremonies is a social expression. For all that, the final validation of the sun dance, as of every other form of Plains religion, seems to rest with the individual in his introspective loneliness. The nuclear idea is the "blessing" or "manitou" experience, in which the individual puts himself in a relation of extreme intimacy with the world of supernatural power or "medicine."

Completely socialized rituals are not the primary fact in the structure of Plains religion; they are rather an extended form of the nuclear individual experience. The recipient of a blessing may and does invite others to participate in the private ritual which has grown up around the vision in which power and security have been vouchsafed to him; he may even transfer his interest in the vision to another individual; in the course of time the original ritual, complicated by many accretions, may become a communal form in which the whole tribe has the most lively and anxious interest, as is the case with the beaver bundle or medicine pipe ceremonies of the Blackfoot Indians. A non-religious individual may see little but show and outward circumstance in all this business of vision and bundle and ritual, but the religious consciousness of the Plains Indians never seems to lose sight of the inherently individual warrant of the vision and of all rituals which may eventually flow from it. It is highly significant that even in the sun dance, which is probably the least individualized kind of religious conduct among these Indians, the high-water mark of religious intensity is felt to reside, not in any collective ecstasy, but in the individual emotions of those who gaze at the center pole of the sun dance lodge and, still more, of the resolute few who are willing to experience the unspeakably painful ecstasy of self-torture.

The Pueblo religion seems to offer very much of a contrast to the religion of the Plains. The Pueblo religion is ritualized to an incredible degree. Ceremony follows relentlessly on ceremony, clan and religious fraternity go through their stately symbolism of dance and prayer and shrine construction with the regularity of the seasons. All is anxious care for the norm and detail of ritual. But is it not the mere bulk of this ritualism which truly characterizes the religion of the Hopi or Zuñi. It is the depersonalized, almost cosmic, quality of the rituals, which have all the air of pre-ordained things of nature which the individual is helpless either to assist or to thwart, and whose mystic intention he can only comprehend by resigning himself to the traditions of his tribe and clan and fraternity. No private intensity of religious experience will help the ritual. Whether the dancer is aroused to a strange ecstasy or remains as cold as an automaton is a matter of perfect indifference to the Pueblo consciousness. All taint of the orgiastic is repudiated by the Pueblo Indian, who is content with the calm constraint and power of things ordained, seeing in himself no discoverer of religious virtue, but only a correct and measured transmitter of things perfect in themselves. One might teach Protestant revivalism to a Blackfoot or a Sioux; a Zuñi would smile uncomprehendingly.

III

Though religion cannot be defined in terms of belief, it is none the less true that the religions of primitive peoples tend to cluster around a number of typical beliefs or classes of belief. It will be quite impossible to give even a superficial account of the many types of religious belief that have been reported for primitive man, and I shall therefore be content with a brief mention of three of them: belief in spirits (animism), belief in gods, and belief in cosmic power (mana).

That primitive peoples are animistic—in other words, that they believe in the existence in the world and in themselves of a vast number of immaterial and potent essences—is a commonplace of anthropology. Tylor attempted to derive all forms of religious behavior from animistic beliefs, and while we can no longer attach as great an importance to animism as did Tylor and others of the classical anthropologists, it is still correct to say that few primitive religions do not at some point or other connect with the doctrine of spirits. Most peoples believe in a soul which animates the human body; some believe in a variety of souls (as when the principle of life is distinguished from what the psychologists would call consciousness of the psyche); and most peoples also believe in the survival of the soul after death in the form of a ghost.

The experiences of the soul or souls typically account for such phenomena as dreams, illness, and death. Frequently one or another type of soul is iden-

tified with such insubstantial things as the breath, or
the shadow cast by a living being, or, more materially, with such parts of the human body as the heart
or diaphragm; sometimes, too, the soul is symbolized
by an imaginary being, such as a mannikin, who
may leave the body and set out in pursuit of another
soul. The mobile soul and the ghost tend to be identified, but this is not necessarily the case.

In all this variety of primitive belief we see little
more than the dawn of psychology. The religious attitude enters in only when the soul or ghost is somehow connected with the great world of non-human
spirits which animates the whole of nature and which
is possessed of a power for good or ill which it is the
constant aim of human beings to capture for their
own purposes. These "spirits," which range all the
way from disembodied human souls, through animals, to god-like creatures, are perhaps more often
feared than directly worshipped. On the whole, it is
perhaps correct to say that spirits touch humanity
through the individual rather than through the
group and that access is gained to them rather
through the private, selfish ritual of magic than
through religion. All such generalizations, however,
are exceedingly dangerous. Almost any association
of beliefs and attitudes is possible.

Tylor believed that the series: soul, ghost, spirit,
god, was a necessary genetic chain. "God" would be
no more than the individualized totality of all spirits,
localized in earth or air or sea and specialized as to
function or kind of power. The single "god" of a pol-
ytheistic pantheon would be the transition stage be-

tween the unindividualized spirit and the Supreme
Being of the great historical religions. These simple
and plausible connections are no longer lightly taken
for granted by the anthropologists. There is a great
deal of disturbing evidence which seems to show
that the idea of a god or of God is not necessarily to
be considered as the result of an evolution of the
idea of soul or spirit. It would seem that some of the
most primitive peoples we know of have arrived at
the notion of an all powerful being who stands quite
outside the world of spirits and who tends to be
identified with such cosmic objects as the sun or the
sky.

The Nootka Indians of British Columbia, for instance, believe in the existence of a Supreme Being
whom they identify with daylight and who is sharply
contrasted both with the horde of mysterious beings
("spirits") from whom they seek power for special
ends and with the mythological beings of legend
and ritual. Some form of primitive monotheism not
infrequently co-exists with animism. Polytheism is
not necessarily the forerunner of monotheism, but
may, for certain culture, be looked upon as a complex, systematized product of several regional ideas
of God.

The idea of "mana," or diffused, non-individual-
ized power, seems to be exceedingly wide-spread
among primitive peoples. The term has been borrowed from Melanesia, but it is as applicable to the
Algonkian, Iroquois, Siouan, and numerous other
tribes of aboriginal America as to the Melanesians
and Polynesians. The whole world is believed to

be pervaded by a mysterious potency that may be
concentrated in particular objects or, in many cases,
possessed by spirits or animals or gods. Man needs
to capture some of this power in order to attain his
desires. He is ever on the lookout for blessings from
the unknown, which may be vouchsafed to him in
unusual or uncanny experiences, in visions, and in
dreams. The notion of immaterial power often takes
curious forms. Thus the Hupa Indians of Northwest-
ern California believe in the presence of radiations
which stream to earth from mysterious realms beyond, inhabited by a supernatural and holy folk who
once lived upon earth but vanished with the coming of the Indians. These radiations may give the
medicine-woman her power or they may inspire one
with the spirit of a ritual.

I can hardly do more than mention some of the
typical forms of religious behavior, as distinguished
from belief, which are of universal distribution.
Prayer is common, but it is only in the higher
reaches of culture that it attains its typically pure
and altruistic form. On lower levels it tends to be
limited to the voicing of selfish wants, which may
even bring harm to those who are not members of
one's own household. It is significant that prayers are
frequently addressed to specific beings who may
grant power or withhold ill rather than to the Supreme Being, even when such a being is believed to
exist.

A second type of religious behavior is the pursuit
of power or "medicine." The forms which this pursuit take are exceedingly varied. The individual

"medicine" experience is perhaps illustrated in its greatest purity among the American aborigines, but it is of course plentifully illustrated in other parts of the world. Among some tribes the receipt of power, which generally takes place in the form of a dream or vision, establishes a very personal relation between the giver of the blessing and the suppliant.

This relation is frequently known as individual totemism. The term totemism, indeed, is derived from the Ojibwa Indians, among whom there is a tendency for the individual to be "blessed" by the same supernatural beings as have already blessed his paternal ancestors. Such an example as this shows how the purely individual relation may gradually become socialized into the institution typically known as totemism, which may be defined as a specific relation, manifested in a great variety of ways, which exists between a clan or other social group and a supernatural being, generally, but by no means exclusively, identified with an animal. In spite of the somewhat shadowy borderland which connects individual totemism with group totemism, it is inadvisable to think of the one institution as necessarily derived from the other, though the possibility of such a development need not be denied outright.

Closely connected with the pursuit of power is the handling of magical objects or assemblages of such objects which contained or symbolize the power that has been bestowed. Among some of the North American Indian tribes, as we have seen, the "medicine bundle," with its associated ritual and taboos, owes its potency entirely to the supernatural experience which lies back of it. Classical fetishism, however, as we find it in West Africa, seems not to be necessarily based on an individual vision. A fetish is an object which possesses power in its own right and which may be used to affect desired ends by appropriate handling, prayer, or other means. In many cases a supernatural being is believed to be actually resident in the fetish, though this conception, which most nearly corresponds to the popular notion of "idol," is probably not as common as might be expected. The main religious significance of medicine bundles, fetishes and other tokens of the supernatural is the reassuring power exerted on the primitive mind by a concrete symbol which is felt to be closely connected with the mysterious unknown and its limitless power. It is of course the persistance of the suggestibility of visual symbols which makes even the highest forms of religion tend to cluster about such objects as temples, churches, shrines, crucifixes, and the like.

The fourth and perhaps the most important of the forms of religious behavior is the carrying out of rituals. Rituals are typically symbolic actions which belong to the whole community, but among primitive peoples there is a tendency for many of them to be looked upon as the special function of a limited group within the whole tribe. Sometimes this group is a clan or gens or other division not based on religious concepts; at other times the group is a religious fraternity, a brotherhood of priests, which exists for the sole purpose of seeing to the correct performance of rituals which are believed to be of the utmost consequence for the safety of the tribe as a whole. It is difficult to generalize about primitive ritual, so varied are the forms which it assumes. Nearly everywhere the communal ritual whips the whole tribe into a state of great emotional tension, which is interpreted by the folk as a visitation from the supernatural world. The most powerful means known to bring about this feeling is the dance, which is nearly always accompanied by singing.

Some ethnologists have seen in primitive ritual little more than the counterpart of our own dramatic and pantomimic performances. Historically there is undoubtedly much truth in this but it would be very misleading to make of a psychology of primitive ritual a mere chapter in the psychology of æsthetic experience. The exaltation of the Sioux sun dancer or of a Northwest Coast Indian who impersonates the Cannibal Spirit is a very different thing from the excitement of the performing artist. It seems very much more akin to the intense revery of the mystic or ascetic. Externally, the ritual may be described as a sacred drama; subjectively, it may bring the participant to a realization of mystery and power for which the fetish or other religious object is but an external token. The psychological interpretation of ritual naturally differs with the temperament of the individual.

IV

The sharp distinction between religious and other modes of conduct to which we are accustomed in modern life is by no means possible on more primitive levels. Religion is neither ethics nor science nor art, but it tends to be inextricably bound up with all three. It also manifests itself in the social organization of the tribe, in ideas of higher or lower status, in the very form and technique of government itself. It is sometimes said that it is impossible to disentangle religious behavior among primitive peoples from the setting in which it is found. For many primitives, however, it seems almost more correct to say that religion is the one structural reality in the whole of their culture and that what we call art and ethics and science and social organization are hardly more than the application of the religious point of view to the functions of daily life.

In concluding, attention may be called to the wide distribution of certain sentiments or feelings which are of a peculiarly religious nature and which tend to persist even among the most sophisticated individuals, long after they have ceased to believe in the rationalized justification for these sentiments and feelings. They are by no means to be identified with simple emotions, though they obviously feed on the soil of all emotions. A religious sentiment is typically unconscious, intense, and bound up with a compulsive sense of values. It is possible that modern psychology may analyze them all away as socialized compulsion neuroses, but it is exceedingly doubtful if a healthy social life or a significant individual life is possible without these very sentiments. The first and most important of them is a "feeling of community with a necessary universe of values." In psychological terms, this feeling seems to be a blend of complete humility and a no less complete security. It is only when the fundamental serenity is as intense as fear and as necessary as of the simpler sentiments that its possessor can be properly termed a mystic.

A second sentiment, which often grows out of the first, is a feeling for sacredness or holiness or divinity. That certain experiences or ideas or objects or personalities must be set apart as symbols of ultimate value is an idea which is repellent to the critical modern mind. It is none the less a necessary sentiment to many, perhaps to most, human beings. The consciously justified infraction of sentiments of holiness, which cannot be recognized by the thinking mind, leads frequently to an inexplicable personal unhappiness.

The taboos of primitive peoples strike us as very bizarre and it is a commonplace of psychoanalysis that many of them have a strange kinship with the apparently self-imposed taboos of neurotics. It is doubtful if many psychologists or students of culture realize the psychological significance of taboo, which seems nothing more nor less than an unconscious striving for the strength that comes from any form of sacrifice or deferment of immediate fulfillments. Certainly all religions have insisted on the importance of both taboo, in its narrower sense of specific interdiction, and sacrifice. It may be that the feeling of the necessity of sacrifice is no more than a translation into action of the sentiment of the holy.

Perhaps the most difficult of the religious sentiments to understand is that of sin, which is almost amusingly abhorrent to the modern mind. Every constellation of sentiments holds within itself its own opposites. The more intense a sentiment, the more certain is the potential presence of a feeling which results from the flouting or thwarting of it. The price for the reality and intensity of the positive sentiments that I have mentioned, any or all of which must of necessity be frequently violated in the course of daily life, is the sentiment of sin, which is a necessary shadow cast by all sincerely religious feeling.

It is, of course, no accident that religion in its most authentic moments has always been prepared to cancel a factual shortcoming in conduct if only it could assure itself that this shortcoming was accompanied by a lively sense of sin. Good works are not the equivalent of the sentiment of ultimate value which religion insists upon. The shadow cast by this sentiment, which is a sense of sin, may be intuitively felt as of more reassuring value than a benevolence which proceeds from mere social habit or from personal indifference. Religion has always been the enemy of self-satisfaction.

Cultural Anthropology
and Psychiatry

Before we try to establish a more intimate relation between the problems of cultural anthropology and those of psychiatry than is generally recognized, it will be well to emphasize the apparent differences of subject matter and purpose which seem to separate them as disciplines concerned with human behavior. In the main, cultural anthropology has emphasized the group and its traditions in contradistinction to individual variations of behavior. It aims to discover the generalized forms of action, thought, and feeling which, in their complex interrelatedness, constitute the culture of a community. Whether the ultimate aim of such a study is to establish a typical sequence of institutional forms in the history of man, or to work out a complete distributional survey of patterns and cultural types over the globe, or to make an exhaustive descriptive analysis of as many cultures as possible in order that fundamental sociological laws may be arrived at, is important, indeed, for the spirit and method of actual research in the field of human culture. But all these approaches agree in thinking of the individual as a more or less passive

Journal of Abnormal and Social Psychology, vol. 27 (1932), 229–242.

carrier of tradition or, to speak more dynamically, as the infinitely variable actualizer of ideas and of modes of behavior which are implicit in the structure and tradition of a given society. It is what all the individuals of a society have in common in their mutual relations which is supposed to constitute the true subject matter of cultural anthropology and sociology. If the testimony of an individual is set down as such, as often happens in our anthropological monographs, it is not because of an interest in the individual himself as a matured and single organism of ideas but in his assumed typicality for the community as a whole.

It is true that there are many statements in our ethnological monographs which, for all that they are presented in general terms, really rest on the authority of a few individuals, or even of one individual, who have had to bear testimony for the group as a whole. Information on kinship systems or rituals or technological processes or details of social organization or linguistic forms is not ordinarily evaluated by the cultural anthropologist as a personal document. He always hopes that the individual informant is near enough to the understandings and intentions of his society to report them duly, thereby implicitly eliminating himself as a factor in the method of research. All realistic field workers in native custom and belief are more or less aware of the dangers of such an assumption and, naturally enough, efforts are generally made to "check up" statements received from single individuals. This is not always possible, however, and so our ethnological monographs present a kaleidoscopic picture of varying degrees of generality, often within the covers of a single volume. Thus, that the Haida Indians of Queen Charlotte Islands were divided into two exogamic phratries, the Eagles and the Ravens, is a statement which could, no doubt, be elicited from any normal Haida Indian. It has very nearly the same degree of impersonality about it that characterizes the statement that the United States is a republic governed by a President. It is true that these data about social and political organization might mean rather different things in the systems of ideas and fantasies of different individuals or might, as master ideas, be construed to lead to typically different forms of action according to whether we studied the behavior of one individual or of another. But that is another matter. The fundamental patterns are relatively clear and impersonal. Yet in many cases we are not so fortunate as in the case of fundamental outlines of political organization or of kinship terminology or of house structure. What shall we do, for instance, with the cosmogenic system of the Bella Coola Indians of British Columbia? The five superimposed worlds which we learn about in this system not only have no close parallels among the other tribes of the Northwest Coast area but have not been vouched for by any informant other than the one individual from whom Boas obtained his information. Is this cosmogenic system typical Bella Coola religious belief? Is it individual fantasy construction or is it a peculiar individual elaboration on the basis of a simpler cosmogenic system which belongs to the community as a whole?

In this special instance the individual note obtrudes itself somewhat embarrassingly. In the main, however, the cultural anthropologist believes or hopes that such disquieting interruptions to the impersonality of his thinking do not occur frequently enough to spoil his science.

Psychiatry is an offshoot of the medical tradition and aims to diagnose, analyze, and, if possible, cure those behavior disturbances of individuals which show to observation as serious deviations from the normal attitude of the individual toward his physical and social environment. The psychiatrist specializes in "mental" diseases as the dermatologist specializes in the diseases of the skin or the gynecologist concerns himself with diseases peculiar to women. The great difference between psychiatry and the other biologically defined medical disciplines is that, while the latter have a definite bodily locus to work with and have been able to define and perfect their methods by diligent exploration of the limited and tangible area of observation assigned to them, psychiatry is apparently doomed to have no more definite locus than the total field of human behavior in its more remote or less immediately organic sense. The conventional companionship of psychiatry and neurology seems to be little more than a declaration of faith by the medical profession that all human ills are, at last analysis, of organic origin and that they are, or should be, localizable in some segment, however complexly defined, of the physiological machine. It is an open secret, however, that the neurologist's science is one thing and the psychiatrist's practice

another. Almost in spite of themselves psychiatrists
have been forced to be content with an elaborate array of clinical pictures, with terminological problems
of diagnosis, and with such thumb rules of clinical
procedure as seem to offer some hope of success in
the handling of actual cases. It is no wonder that psychiatry tends to be distrusted by its sister disciplines
within the field of medicine and that the psychiatrists
themselves, worried by a largely useless medical
training and secretly exasperated by their inability
to apply the strictly biological part of their training
to their peculiar problems, tend to magnify the importance of the biological approach in order that
they may not feel that they have strayed away
from the companionship of their more illustrious
brethren. No wonder that the more honest and sensitive psychiatrists have come to feel that the trouble lies not so much in psychiatry itself as in the role
which general medicine has wished psychiatry to
play.

Those insurgent psychiatrists, among whom Freud
must be reckoned the most courageous and the most
fertile in ideas, have come to feel that many of the
so-called nervous and mental disorders can be
looked upon as the logical development of systems
of ideas and feelings which have grown up in the
experience of the individual and which have an unconscious value for him as the symbolic solution of
profound difficulties that arise in an effort to adjust
to his human environment. The morbidity, in other
words, that the psychiatrist has to deal with seems,
for the most part, to be not a morbidity of organic

segments or even of organic functions but of experience itself. His attempts to explain a morbid suspiciousness of one's companions or delusion as to one's status in society by some organically definable weakness of the nervous system or of the functioning of the endocrine glands may be no more to the point than to explain the habit of swearing by the absence of a few teeth or by a poorly shaped mouth. This is not the place to go into an explanation, however brief, of the new points of view which are to be credited to Freud and his followers and which have invaded the thinking of even the most conservative of psychiatrists to no inconsiderable extent. All that interests us here is to note the fact that psychiatry is moving away from its historic position of a medical discipline that is chronically unable to make good to that of a discipline that is medical only by tradition and courtesy and is compelled, with or without permission, to attack fundamental problems of psychology and sociology so far as they affect the well-being of the individual. The locus, then, of psychiatry turns out not to be the human organism at all in any fruitful sense of the word but the more intangible, and yet more intelligible, world of human relationships and ideas that such relationships bring forth. Those students of medicine who see in these trends little more than a return to the old mythology of the "soul" are utterly unrealistic, for they tacitly assume that all experience is but the mechanical sum of physiological processes lodged in isolated individuals. This is no more defensible a position than the naïvely metaphysical contention that a table or chair or hat or church can be intelligibly defined in terms of their molecular and atomic constitution. That A hates B or hopelessly loves B or is jealous of B or is mortally afraid of B or hates him in one respect and loves him in another can result only from the complications of experience. If we work out a gradually complicating structure of morbid relationships between A and B and, by successive transfers, between A or B and the rest of the human world, we discover behavior patterns that are none the less real and even tragic for not being fundamentally attributable to some weakness or malfunctioning of the nervous system or any other part of the organism. This does not mean that weakness or malfunctioning of a strictly organic character may not result from a morbidity of human relationships. Such an organic theory would be no more startling than to maintain that a chronic sneer may disfigure the shape of the mouth or that a secret fear may impair one's digestion. There are, indeed, signs that psychiatry, slowly and painfully delivering itself from the somatic superstitions of medicine, may take its revenge by attempts to "mentalize" large sections of medical theory and practice. The future, alone can tell how much of these psychological interpretations of organic disease is sound doctrine or a new mythology.

There is reason, then, to think that while cultural anthropology and psychiatry have distinct problems to begin with, they must, at some point, join hands in a highly significant way. That culture is a superorganic, impersonal whole is a useful enough methodological principle to begin with but becomes a serious deterrent in the long run to the more dynamic study of the genesis and development of cultural patterns because these cannot be realistically disconnected from those organizations of ideas and feelings which constitute the individual. The ultimate methodological error of the student of personality is perhaps less obvious than the correlative error of the student of culture but is all the more insidious and dangerous for that reason. Mechanisms which are unconsciously evolved by the neurotic or psychotic are by no means closed systems imprisoned within the biological walls of isolated individuals. They are tacit commentaries on the validity or invalidity of some of the more intimate implications of culture for the adjustment processes of given individuals. We are not, therefore, to begin with a simple contrast between social patterns and individual behavior, whether normal or abnormal, but we are, rather, to ask what is the meaning of culture in terms of individual behavior and whether the individual can, in a sense, be looked upon as the effective carrier of the culture of his group. As we follow tangible problems of behavior rather than the selected problems set by recognized disciplines, we discover the field of social psychology, which is not a whit more social than it is individual and which is, or should be, the mother science from which stem both the abstracted impersonal problems as phrased by the cultural anthropologist and the almost impertinently realistic explorations into behavior which are the province of the psychiatrist. Be it remarked in passing that what passes for individual psychology is little more than an ill-assorted mélange of bits of physiology and of studies of highly fragmentary modes of behavior which have been artificially induced by the psychologist. This abortive discipline seems to be able to arrive at no integral conceptions of either individual or society and one can only hope that it will eventually surrender all its problems to physiology and social psychology.

Cultural anthropology has not been neglected by psychiatry. The psychoanalysts in particular have made very extensive use of the data of cultural anthropology in order to gather evidence in support of their theories of the supposed "racial inheritance of ideas" by the individual. Neurotic and psychotic, through the symbolic mechanisms which control their thinking, are believed to regress to a more primitive state of mental adjustment than is normal in modern society and which is supposed to be preserved for our observation in the institutions of primitive peoples. In some undefined way which it seems quite impossible to express in intelligible biological or psychological terms the cultural experiences which have been accumulated by primitive man are believed to be unconsciously handed on to his more civilized progeny. The resemblances between the content of primitive ritual—and symbolic behavior generally among primitive peoples—and the apparently private rituals and symbolisms developed by those who have greater than normal difficulty in adjusting to their social environment are said to be so numerous and far-reaching that the latter must be looked upon as an inherited survival of more archaic types of thought and feeling. Hence, we are told, it is very useful to study the culture of primitive man, for in this way an enormous amount of light is thrown upon the fundamental significance of modes of behavior in the neurotic which are otherwise inexplicable. The searching clinical investigation into the symbolisms of the neurotic recovers for us, on a modern and highly disguised level, what lies but a little beneath the surface among the primitives, who are still living under an archaic psychological régime.

Psychoanalysts welcome the contributions of cultural anthropology but it is exceedingly doubtful if many cultural anthropologists welcome the particular spirit in which the psychoanalysts appreciate their data. The cultural anthropologist can make nothing of the hypothesis of the racial unconscious nor is he disposed to allow an immediate psychological analysis of the behavior of primitive people in any other sense than that in which such an analysis is allowable for our own culture. He believes that it is as illegitimate to analyze totemism or primitive laws of inheritance or set rituals in terms of the peculiar symbolisms discovered or invented by the psychoanalyst as it would be to analyze the most complex forms of modern social behavior in these terms. And he is disposed to think that if the resemblances between the neurotic and the primitive which have so often been pointed out are more than fortuitous, it is not because of a cultural atavism which the neurotic exemplifies but simply because all human beings, whether primitive or sophisticated in the cultural sense, are, at rock bottom, psychologically primitive, and there is no reason why a significant unconscious symbolism which gives substitutive satisfaction to the individual may not become socialized on any level of human activity.

The service of cultural anthropology to psychiatry is not as mysterious or remote or clandestine as psychoanalytic mysticism would have us believe. It is of a much simpler and healthier sort. It lies very much nearer the surface of things than is generally believed. Cultural anthropology, if properly understood, has the healthiest of all scepticisms about the validity of the concept "normal behavior." It cannot deny the useful tyranny of the normal in a given society but it believes the external form of normal adjustment to be an exceedingly elastic thing. It is very doubtful if the normalities of any primitive society that lies open to inspection are nearer the hypothetical responses of an archaic type of man, untroubled by a burdensome historical past, than the normalities of a modern Chinese or Scotchman. In specific instances one may even wonder whether they are not tangibly less so. It would be more than a joke to turn the tables and to suggest that the psychoanalysis of an over-ritualized Pueblo Indian or Toda might denude him sufficiently to set him "regressing" to the psychologically primitive status of an American professor's child or a professor himself. The cultural anthropologist's quarrel with psychoanalysis can perhaps be put most significantly by pointing out that the psychoanalyst has confused the archaic in the conceptual or theoretical psychologic sense with the archaic in the literal chronological sense. Cultural anthropology is not valuable because it uncovers the archaic in the psychological sense. It is valuable because it is constantly rediscovering the normal. For the psychiatrist and for the student of personality in general this is of the greatest importance, for personalities are not conditioned by a generalized process of adjustment to "the normal" but by the necessity of adjusting to the greatest possible variety of idea patterns and action patterns according to the accidents of birth and biography.

The so-called culture of a group of human beings, as it is ordinarily treated by the cultural anthropologist, is essentially a systematic list of all the socially inherited patterns of behavior which may be illustrated in the actual behavior of all or most of the individuals of the group. The true locus, however, of these processes which, when abstracted into a totality, constitute culture is not in a theoretical community of human beings known as society, for the term "society" is itself a cultural construct which is employed by individuals who stand in significant relations to each other in order to help them in the interpretation of certain aspects of their behavior. The true locus of culture is in the interactions of specific individuals and, on the subjective side, in the world of meanings which each one of these individuals may unconsciously abstract for himself from his participation in these interactions. Every individual is, then, in a very real sense, a representative of at least one sub-culture which may be abstracted from the generalized culture of the group of which he is a member. Frequently, if not typically, he is a representative of more than one sub-culture, and the degree to which the socialized behavior of any given individual can be identified with or abstracted from the typical or generalized culture of a single group varies enormously from person to person.

It is impossible to think of any cultural pattern or set of cultural patterns which can, in the literal sense of the word, be referred to society as such. There are no facts of political organization or family life or religious belief or magical procedure or technology or aesthetic endeavor which are coterminous with society or with any mechanically or sociologically defined segment of society. The fact that John Doe is registered in some municipal office as a member of such and such a ward only vaguely defines him with reference to those cultural patterns which are conveniently assembled under some such term as "municipal administration." The psychological and, in the deepest sense of the word, the cultural realities of John Doe's registration may, and do, vary enormously. If John Doe is paying taxes on a house which is likely to keep him a resident of the ward for the rest of his life and if he also happens to be in personal contact with a number of municipal officers, ward classification may easily become a symbol of his orientation in his world of meanings which is comparable for clarity, if not for importance, to his definition as a father of a family or as a frequent participant in golf. Ward membership, for such an individual, may easily precipitate itself into many visible forms of behavior. The ward system and its functions, real or supposed, may for such a John

Doe assume an impersonal and objective reality which is comparable to the objective reality of rain or sunshine.

But there is sure to be another John Doe, perhaps a neighbor of the first, who does not even know that the town is divided into wards and that he is, by definition, enrolled in one of them and that he has certain duties and privileges connected with such enrollment, whether he cares to exercise them or not. While the municipal office classifies these two John Does in exactly the same way and while there is a theory on foot that ward organization, with its associated functions, is an entirely impersonal matter to which all members of a given society must adjust, it is rather obvious that such a manner of speech is little more than a sociological metaphor. The cultures of these two individuals are, as a matter of fact, significantly different, as significantly different, on the given level and scale, as though one were the representative of Italian culture and the other of Turkish culture. Such differences of culture never seem as significant as they really are; partly because in the workaday world of experience they are not often given the opportunity to emerge into sharp consciousness, partly because the economy of interpersonal relations and the friendly ambiguities of language conspire to reinterpret for each individual all behavior which he has under observation in the terms of those meanings which are relevant to his own life. The concept of culture, as it is handled by the cultural anthropologist, is necessarily something of a statistical fiction and it is easy to see that the social psychologist and the psychiatrist must eventually induce him to reconsider carefully his terms. It is not the concept of culture which is subtly misleading but the metaphysical locus to which culture is generally assigned.

Clearly, not all cultural traits are of equal importance for the development of personality, for not all of them are equally diffused as integral elements in the idea-systems of different individuals. Some modes of behavior and attitude are pervasive and compelling beyond the power of even the most isolated individual to withstand or reject. Such patterns would be, for example, the symbolisms of affection or hostility; the overtones of emotionally significant words; certain fundamental implications and many details of the economic order; much, but by no means all, of those understandings and procedures which constitute the law of the land. Patterns of this kind are compulsive for the vast majority of human beings but the degree of compulsiveness is in no simple relation to the official, as contrasted with the inner or psychological, significance of these patterns. Thus, the use of an offensive word may be of negligible importance from a legal standpoint but may, psychologically considered, have an attracting or repelling potency that far transcends the significance of so serious a behavior pattern as, say, embezzlement or the nature of one's scientific thinking. A culture as a whole cannot be said to be adequately known for purposes of personality study until the varying degrees of compulsiveness which attach to its many aspects and implications are rather definitely understood. No doubt there are cultural patterns which tend to be universal, not only in form but in psychological significance, but it is very easy to be mistaken in those matters and to impute equivalences of meaning which do not truly exist.

There are still other cultural patterns which are real and compelling only for special individuals or groups of individuals and are as good as non-existent for the rest of the group. Such, for instance, are the ideas, attitudes, and modes of behavior which belong to specialized trades. We are all aware of the reality of such private or limited worlds of meaning. The dairy-man, the movie actress, the laboratory physicist, the party whip, have obviously built up worlds which are anonymous or opaque to each other or, at best, stand to each other in a relation of blanket acceptance. There is much tacit mythology in such hugely complex societies as our own which makes it possible for the personal significance of sub-cultures to be overlooked. For each individual, the commonly accepted fund of meanings and values tends to be powerfully specialized or emphasized or contradicted by types of experience and modes of interpretation that are far from being the property of all men. If we consider that these specialized cultural participations are partly the result of contact with limited traditions and techniques, partly the result of identification with such biologically and socially imposed groups as the family or the class in school or the club, we can begin to see how inevitable it is that the true psychological locus of *a* culture is *the individual* or *a specifically enumerated list of individuals,* not an economically or politically or socially defined group of individuals. "Individual," however, here means not simply a biologically defined organism maintaining itself through physical impacts and symbolic substitutes of such impacts, but that total world of form, meaning, and implication of symbolic behavior which a given individual partly knows and directs, partly intuits and yields to, partly is ignorant of and is swayed by.

Still other cultural patterns have neither a generalized nor a specialized potency. They may be termed marginal or referential and while they may figure as conceptually important in the scheme of a cultural theorist, they may actually have little or no psychological importance for the normal human being. Thus, the force of linguistic analogy which creates the plural "unicorns" is a most important force for the linguistic analyst to be clear about, but it obvious that the psychological imminence of that force, while perfectly real, may be less than the avoidance, say, of certain obscene or impolite words, an avoidance which the linguist, in turn, may quite legitimately look upon as marginal to his sphere of interests. In the same way, while such municipal subdivisions as wards are, from the standpoint of political theory, of the same order as state lines and even national lines, they are not psychologically so. They are psychologically related to such saturated entities as New York or "the South" or Fifth Avenue or "the slums" as undeveloped property in the suburbs is economically related to real estate in the business heart of a great metropolis.

Some of this marginal cultural property is held as marginal by the vast majority of participants in the total culture, if we may still speak in terms of a "total culture." Others of these marginal patterns are so only for certain individuals or groups of individuals. No doubt, to a movie actress the intense world of values which engages the participation of a physicist tends to be marginal in about the same sense as a legal fiction or unactualized linguistic possibility may be marginal cultural property. A "hard-headed business man" may consign the movie actress and the physicist to two adjoining sectors, "lively" and "sleepy" respectively, of a marginal tract of "triviality." Culture, then, varies infinitely, not only as to manifest content but as to the distribution of psychologic emphases on the elements and implications of this content. According to our scale of treatment, we have to deal with the cultures of groups and the cultures of individuals.

A personality is carved out by the subtle interaction of those systems of ideas which are characteristic of the culture as a whole, as well as of those systems of ideas which get established for the individual through more special types of participation, with the physical and psychological needs of the individual organism, which cannot take over any of the cultural material that is offered in its original form but works it over more or less completely, so that it integrates with those needs. The more closely we study this interaction, the more difficult it becomes to distinguish society as a cultural and psychological unit from the individual who is thought

of as a member of the society to whose culture he is
required to adjust. No problem of social psychology
that is at all realistic can be phrased by starting with
the conventional contrast of the individual and his
society. Nearly every problem of social psychology
needs to consider the exact nature and implication
of an idea complex, which we may look upon as the
psychological correlate of the anthropologist's cultural pattern, to work out its relation to other idea
complexes and what modifications it necessarily
undergoes as it accommodates itself to these, and,
above all, to ascertain the precise locus of such a
complex. This locus is rarely identifiable with society
as a whole, except in a purely philosophical or conceptual sense, nor is it often lodged in the psyche
of a single individual. In extreme cases such an idea
complex or cultural pattern may be the dissociated
segment of a single individual's mind or it may
amount to no more than a potential revivification of
ideas in the mind of a single individual through the
aid of some such symbolic depositary as a book or
museum. Ordinarily the locus will be a substantial
portion of the members of a community, each of
them feeling that he is touching common interests
so far as this particular culture pattern is concerned.
We have learned that the individual in isolation
from society is a psychological fiction. We have not
had the courage to face the fact that formally organized groups are equally fictitious in the psychological
sense, for geographically contiguous groups are
merely a first approximation to the infinitely variable groupings of human beings to whom culture

in its various aspects is actually to be credited as a matter of realistic psychology.

"Adjustment," as the term is ordinarily understood, is a superficial concept because it regards only the end product of individual behavior as judged from the standpoint of the requirements, real or supposed, of a particular society. In reality "adjustment" consists of two distinct and even conflicting types of process. It includes, obviously, those accommodations to the behavior requirements of the group without which the individual would find himself isolated and ineffective, but it includes, just as significantly, the effort to retain and make felt in the opinions and attitudes of others that particular cosmos of ideas and values which has grown up more or less unconsciously in the experience of the individual. Ideally these two adjustment tendencies need to be compromised into behavior patterns which do justice to both requirements.

It is a dangerous thing for the individual to give up his identification with such cultural patterns as have come to symbolize for him his own personality integration. The task of external adjustment to social needs may require such abandonment on his part and consciously he may crave nothing more passionately, but if he does not wish to invite disharmony and inner weakness in his personality, he must see to it, consciously or unconsciously, that every abandonment is made good by the acquisition of a psychologically equivalent symbolism. External observations on the adjustment processes of individuals are often highly misleading as to their psychological significance. The usual treatment, for instance, of behavior tendencies known as radical and conservative must leave the genuine psychiatrist cold because he best realizes that the same types of behavior, judged externally, may have entirely distinct, even contradictory, meanings for different individuals. One may be a conservative out of fear or out of superb courage. A radical may be such because he is so secure in his fundamental psychic organization as to have no fear for the future, or, on the contrary, his courage may be merely the fantasied rebound from fear of the only too well known.

Strains which are due to this constant war of adjustment are by no means of equal intensity for all individuals. Systems of ideas grew up in endless ways, both within a so-called uniform culture and through the blending of various aspects of so-called distinct cultures, and very different symbolisms and value emphases necessarily arise in the endless subcultures or private symbol organizations of the different members of a group. This is tantamount to saying that certain systems of ideas are more perilously exposed to the danger of disintegration than others. Even if it be granted, as no one would seriously argue that it should not, that individual differences of an inherited sort are significantly responsible for mental breakdowns, it yet remains true that such a "failure" in the life of an individual cannot be completely understood by the study, however minute, of the individual's body and mind as such. Such a failure invites a study of his system of ideas as a more or less distinct cultural entity which has been vainly striving to maintain itself in a discouraging environment.

We may go so far as to suggest quite frankly that a psychosis, for instance, may be an index at one and the same time of the too great resistance of the individual to the forces that play upon him and, so far as *his* world of values is concerned, of the cultural poverty of his psychological environment. The more obvious conflicts of cultures with which we are familiar in the modern world create an uneasiness which forms a fruitful soil for the eventual development, in particular cases, of neurotic symptoms and mental breakdowns but they can hardly be considered sufficient to account for serious psychological derangements. These arise not on the basis of a generalized cultural conflict but out of specific conflicts of a more intimate sort, in which systems of ideas get attached to particular persons, or images of such persons, who play a decisive role in the life of the individual as representative of cultural values.

The personal meanings of the symbolisms of an individual's sub-culture are constantly being reaffirmed by society or, at the least, he likes to think that they are. When they obviously cease to be, he loses his orientation and that strange instinct, or whatever we call it, which in the history of culture has always tended to preserve a system of ideas from destruction, causes his alienation from an impossible world. Both the psychosis and the development of an idea or institution through the centuries manifest the stubbornness of idea complexes and their implications in the face of a material environment which is less demanding psychologically than physically. The mere problem of biological adjustment, or even of ego adjustment as it is ordinarily handled by the sociologist, is comparatively simple. It is literally true that "man wants but little here below nor wants that little long." The trouble always is that he wants that little on his own terms. It is not enough to satisfy one's material wants, to have success in one's practical endeavors, to give and receive affection, or to accomplish any of the purposes laid down by psychologists and sociologists and moralists. Personality organizations, which at last analysis are psychologically comparable with the greatest cultures or idea systems, have as their first law of being their essential self-preservation, and all conscious attempts to define their functions or to manipulate their intention and direction are but the estimable rationalization of people who are wanting to "do things." Modern psychiatrists should be tolerant not only of varying personalities but of the different types of values which personality variations imply. Psychiatrists who are tolerant only in the sense that they refrain from criticizing anybody who is subjected to their care and who do their best to guide him back to the renewed performance of society's rituals may be good practical surgeons of the psyche. They are not necessarily the profoundly sympathetic students of the mind who respect the fundamental intent and direction of every personality organization.

Perhaps it is not too much to expect that a number of gifted psychiatrists may take up the serious study of exotic and primitive cultures, not in the spirit of meretricious voyaging in behalf of Greenwich Village nor to collect an anthology of psychoanalytic fairy tales, but in order to learn to understand, more fully than we can out of the resources of our own cultures, the development of ideas and symbols and their relevance for the problem of personality.

Personality

The term personality is too variable in usage to be serviceable in scientific discussion unless its meaning is very carefully defined for a given context. Among the various understandings which attach to the term there are five definitions which stand out as usefully distinct from one another, corresponding to the philosophical, the physiological, the psychophysical, the sociological and the psychiatric approaches to personality. As a philosophical concept, personality may be defined as the subjective awareness of the self as distinct from other objects of observation. As a purely physiological concept, personality may be considered as the individual human organism with emphasis on those aspects of behavior which differentiate it from other human organisms. The term may be used in a descriptive psychophysical sense as referring to the human being conceived as a given totality, at any one time, of physiological and psychological reaction systems, no vain attempt being made to draw a line between the physiological and the psychological. The most useful sociological connotation which can be given to the term is an essentially symbolic one; namely, the totality of those aspects of behavior which give meaning to an indi-

Encyclopaedia of the Social Sciences (New York, The Macmillan Company, 1934), vol. 12, pp. 85–87.

vidual in society and differentiate him from other members in the community, each of whom embodies countless cultural patterns in a unique configuration. The psychiatric definition of personality may be regarded as equivalent to the individual abstracted from the actual psychophysical whole and conceived as a comparatively stable system of reactivity. The philosophical concept treats personality as an invariant point of experience; the physiological and psychophysical, as an indefinitely variable reactive system, the relation between the sequence of states being one of continuity, not identity; the sociological, as a gradually cumulative entity; and the psychiatric, as an essentially invariant reactive system.

The first four meanings add nothing new to such terms as self or ego, organism, individual and social role. It is the peculiarly psychiatric conception of personality as a reactive system which is in some sense stable or typologically defined for a long period of time, perhaps for life, which it is most difficult to assimilate but important to stress. The psychiatrist does not deny that the child who rebels against his father is in many significant ways different from the same individual as a middle aged adult who has a penchant for subversive theories, but he is interested primarily in noting that the same reactive ground plan, physical and psychic, can be isolated from the behavior totalities of child and adult. He establishes his invariance of personality by a complex system of concepts of behavior equivalences, such as sublimation, affective transfer, rationalization, libido and ego relations. The stage in the history of the human organisms at which it is most convenient to consider the personality as an achieved system, from which all subsequent cross sections of individual psycho-physical history may be measured as minor or even irrelevant variations, is still undetermined. There is no way of telling how far back in the life of the individual the concept of an essentially invariant reactive system may usefully be pushed without too disturbing a clash with the manifest and apparently unlimited variability of individual behavior. If this conception of personality is to hold its own, it must in some way contradict effectively the notion of that cumulative growth of personality to which our practical intelligence must chiefly be directed. The psychiatrist's concept of personality is to all intents and purposes the reactive system exhibited by the precultural child, a total configuration of reactive tendencies determined by heredity, and by prenatal and postnatal conditioning up to the point where cultural patterns are constantly modifying the child's behavior. The personality may be conceived of as a latent system of reaction patterns and tendencies to reaction patterns finished shortly after birth or well into the second or third year of the life of the individual. With all the uncertainty that now prevails with regard to the relative permanence or modifiability of life patterns in the individual and in the race it is unwise, however, to force the notion of the fixation of personality in time.

The genesis of personality is in all probability determined largely by the anatomical and physiological make-up of the individual but cannot be entirely so explained. Conditioning factors, which may roughly be lumped together as the social psychological determinants of childhood, must be considered as at least as important in the development of personality as innate biological factors. It is entirely vain in the present state of knowledge to argue as to the relative importance of these two sets of factors. No satisfactory technique has been developed for keeping them apart and it is perhaps safe to take for granted *hat there is no facet of personality, however minute, which is not from the genetic standpoint the result of the prolonged and subtle interplay of both.

It is unthinkable that the build and other physical characteristics of an individual should bear no relation to his personality. It is important to observe, however, that physical features may be of genetic significance in two distinct respects. They may be organically correlated with certain psychological features or tendencies or they may serve as consciously or unconsciously evaluated symbols of an individual's relation to others, belonging properly to the sphere of social determination. An example of the former class of physical determinants would be the association, according to Kretschmer, of the stocky, so-called pyknic, build, with the cyclothymic type of personality, which in its psychotic form shows as manic depressive insanity, the so-called asthenic and athletic builds being associated with the schizothymic type of personality, which, under the pressure of shock and conflict, may disintegrate into schizophrenia. An example of the latter type of determination, stressed by Alfred Adler and his school of individual psychology, would be the feeling of secret inferiority produced in a person who is of abnormally short stature, and the ceaseless effort to overcome this feeling of inferiority by developing such compensatory mechanisms as intelligent aggression or shrewdness, which would tend to give the individual a secondary ego satisfaction denied him by his sense of physical inferiority. It is highly probable that both of these genetic theories of personality have a substantial core of value although too much has doubtless been claimed for them.

The most elaborate and far reaching hypotheses on the development of personality which have yet been proposed are those of Freud and his school. The Freudian psychoanalysts analyze the personality topographically into a primary id, the sum of inherited impulses or cravings; the ego, which is thought of as being built upon the id through the progressive development of the sense of external reality; and the super-ego, the socially conditioned sum of forces which restrain the individual from the direct satisfaction of the id. The characteristic interplay of these personality zones, itself determined chiefly by the special pattern of family relationships into which the individual has had to fit himself in the earliest years of his life, is responsible for a variety of personality types. Freudians have not developed a systematic theory of personality types but have contented themselves with special hypotheses based on clinical evidence. There is no doubt that a large amount of valuable material and a number of powerfully suggestive mechanisms of personality formation have been advanced by the Freudian school. Even now it is abundantly clear that an unusual attachment to the mother or profound jealously of the older or younger brother may give the personality a slant which remains relatively fixed throughout life.

Various classifications of personality types have been advanced, some of them based on innate factors, others on experiential ones. Among the typological pictures the one worthy of special note is perhaps that of Jung. To him may be attributed the popular contrast between introverts and extraverts, the former abstracting more readily from reality and finding their sense of values and personal identification within themselves, while the latter evaluate experience in terms of what is immediately given by the environment. This contrast, it is true, means something substantial, but it is unfortunate that a host of superficial psychologists have attempted to fix Jung's meaning with the aid of shallow criteria of all sorts. Jung further divides personality into four main functional types—thinking, feeling, sensational and intuitive—the two former being called rational, the two latter irrational. For these somewhat misleading terms, organized and unorganized may fitly be substituted. The classification according to functional types is believed by Jung to intercross with the introvert-extravert dichotomy. The validity and exact delimitation of these terms present many difficult problems of analysis. There is much that is suggestive in his classification of personality and it may be possible to integrate it with the dynamic theories of Freud and Adler. What is needed at the present time, however, is the ever more minute analysis and comparison of individual personality pictures.

There is an important relation between culture and personality. On the one hand, there can be little doubt that distinctive personality types may have a profound influence on the thought and action of the community as a whole. Furthermore, while cultural anthropologists and sociologists do not consider that the forms of social interaction are in themselves definitive of personality types, particular forms of behavior in society, however flexibly the individual may adapt himself to them, are preferentially adapted to specific personality types. Aggressive military patterns, for instance, cannot be equally congenial to all personalities; literary or scientific refinement can be developed only by individuals of highly differentiated personalities. The failure of social science as a whole to relate the patterns of culture to germinal personality patterns is intelligible in view of the complexity of social phenomena and the recency of serious speculation on the relation of the individual to society. But there is growing recognition of the fact that the intimate study of personality is of fundamental concern to the social scientist.

The socialization of personality traits may be expected to lead cumulatively to the development of specific psychological biases in the cultures of the world. Thus Eskimo culture, contrasted with most North American Indian cultures, is extraverted; Hindu culture on the whole corresponds to the world of the thinking introvert; the culture of the United States is definitely extraverted in character, with a greater emphasis on thinking and intuition than on feeling; and sensational evaluations are more clearly evident in the cultures of the Mediterranean area than in those of northern Europe. Social scientists have been hostile to such psychological characterizations of culture but in the long run they are inevitable and necessary.

Psychiatric and Cultural Pitfalls in the Business of Getting a Living

All special sciences of man's physical and cultural nature tend to create a framework of tacit assumptions which enable their practitioners to work with maximum economy and generality. The classical example of this unavoidable tendency is the science of economics, which is too intent on working out a general theory of value, production, flow of commodities, demand, price, to take time to inquire seriously into the nature and variability of those fundamental biological and psychological determinants of behavior which make these economic terms meaningful in the first place. The sum total of the tacit assumptions of a biological and psychological nature which economics makes get petrified into a standardized conception of "economic man," who is endowed with just those motivations which make the known facts of economic behavior in our society seem natural and inevitable. In this way the economist gradually develops a peculiarly powerful insensitiveness to actual motivations, substituting life-like fictions for the troublesome contours of life itself.

The economist is not in the least exceptional in his

Mental Health, Publication No. 9 (American Association for the Advancement of Science, 1939), pp. 237–244.

unconscious procedure. Any one who deals habitually with what man makes and thinks, not because he is interested in man directly but because he wishes to find law and order in what man makes and thinks, slips, by insensible degrees, into the assumption that such regularities of form and process as he finds in selected categories of man's behavior are fundamentally due to a peculiar quality of self-determination in those categories rather than to the ceaseless, eternally shifting, balancing of concretely definable motivations of particular people at particular times and in particular places. The very terminology which is used by the many kinds of segmental scientists of man indicates how remote man himself has become as a necessary concept in the methodology of the respective sciences. Thus, in economics, one speaks of "the flow of commodities," without special concern for a close factual analysis of modifications of demand which, if studied in their full realism, might be shown to be due to such factors as hatred of an alien group, growth of superstition, increased interest in bawdy shows, or decline of prestige of hotel life, each of these motivational categories, in turn, opening up a series of inquiries into intricate problems of interpersonal relations, direct and symbolic. In aesthetics, one can speak of "necessary balances of lines or tone masses" almost as though one were the Demiurge of the universe in whispered conversation with the law of gravitation, apparently without a suspicion that defects of eye and ear structure or highly indirect imputations of "meaning" due to the vacillations of fashion have anything to do with the "aesthetic" problem of how to create "satisfactory balances" of an "aesthetic order." In linguistics, abstracted speech sounds, words and the arrangement of words have come to have so authentic a vitality that one can speak of "regular sound changes" and "loss of genders" without knowing or caring who opened their mouths, at what time, to communicate what to whom.

SCIENCE VS. MAN

The purpose of these remarks is simply to indicate that science itself, when applied to the field of normal human interest, namely man and his daily concerns, creates a serious difficulty for those of us who find it profitable to envisage a true "psychiatric science" or "science of interpersonal relations."[1] The

---

[1] As some of my readers have from time to time expressed their difficulty with my non-medical use of the terms "psychiatry" and "psychiatric," I must explain that I use these terms in lieu of a possible use of "psychology" and "psychological" with explicit stress on the total personality as the central point of reference in all problems of behavior and in all problems of "culture" (analysis of socialized patterns). Thus, a segmental behavior study, such as a statistical inquiry into the ability of children of the age group 7–11 to learn to read, is not in my sense a properly "psychiatric" study because the attention is focused on a fundamentally arbitrary objective, however important or interesting, one not directly suggested by the study of personality structure and the relations of defined personalities to each other. Such a study may be referred to "psychology" or "applied psychology" or "education" or "educational psychology." Equally marginal to "psychiatry" in my sense is such a study in the externalized patterning of "collective behavior" as the analysis of a ritual or handicraft, whether descriptively or historically. Studies of this type may be referred to "ethnology" or "culture history" or "sociology."

On the other hand, a systematic study of the acquirement of

nature of this difficulty may be defined as follows. Inasmuch as science has greater prestige in our serious thinking than daily observation, however shrewd or accurate, or than those obscure convictions about human beings which result from a ceaseless experiencing of them, there tends to grow up in the minds of the vast majority of us a split between two kinds of "knowledge" about man. Every fragmentary science of man, such as economics or political science or aesthetics or linguistics, needs at least a minimum set of assumptions about the nature of man in order to house the particular propositions and records of events which belong to its selected domain. These fragmentary pictures of man are not in intelligible or relevant accord with each other nor do they, when wilfully integrated by a sort of philosophic fiat, give us anything remotely resembling the tightly organized and fatefully moving individuals that we cannot but know and understand up to a certain point,

reading habits with reference to whether they help or hinder the development of fantasy in children of defined personality type is a properly "psychiatric" study because the concept of the total personality is necessarily utilized in it. A close study of the symbolisms of ritual or handicraft, provided these symbolisms are discussed as having immediate relevance for our understanding personality types, is also a truly "psychiatric" study. "Personology" and "personalistic" would be adequate terms but are too uncouth for practical use. My excuse for extending the purely "medical" connotation of the terms "psychiatry" and "psychiatric" is that psychiatrists themselves, in trying to understand the wherefore of aberrant behavior, have had to look far more closely into basic problems of personality structure, of symbolism, and of fundamental human interrelationships than have either the "psychologists" or the various types of "social scientists."

however much it may be to our advantage not to know and understand them at all. A student of aesthetics finds it very much to his advantage to make certain sweeping assumptions about the "aesthetic nature" of man in order to give himself maximum clearance for the development of those propositions and for the record and explanation of those events which professionally interest him, those that work with him and those that have preceded him in a prestige-laden tradition. Random observations about "beautiful" things or structures, such as arrangements of ideas, such observations as might be made by a child or by any naïve person who cannot define aesthetic terms and who has no conscious place for them in that personally useful vocabulary which defines his universe, tend to be dismissed as marginal to the proper concern of aesthetics, as untutored, as of impure conceptual manufacture. The aesthetician is amused or annoyed, as the case may be. He has to be almost a genius to be instructed. The less fateful is the split between his professional conception of man as a beauty-discerning and beauty-creating organism and his humble perceptions of man as a psychobiological organism, the less difficulty will he have to surrender the rigid outlines of his science to the fate of all historical constructs. Such a synthetist is secretly grateful for anything that jars him out of the certainties and necessities of his ghost-inhabited science and brings him back to the conditionalities of an experience that was too hastily and magnificently integrated ("cured," the psychiatrist might say) by his science in the first place.

It is not really difficult, then, to see why anyone brought up on the austerities of a well-defined science of man must, if he is to maintain his symbolic self-respect, become more and more estranged from man himself. Economic laws become more "real" than certain people who try to make a living; the necessities of the "State" get to outweigh in conceptual urgency the desire of the vast majority of human beings to be bothered as little as possible; the laws of syntax acquire a higher reality than the immediate reality of the stammerer who is trying to "get himself across"; the absolute beauty, or lack of it, of an isolated picture or isolated poem becomes a mere insistent item in the diary of the cosmos than the mere fact of whether there is anybody around who is moved by it or not.

Now fantasied universes of self-contained meaning are the very finest and noblest substitutes we can ever devise for that precise and loving insight into the nooks and crannies of the real that must be forever denied us. But we must not reverse the arrow of experience and claim for experience's imaginative condensations the primacy in an appeal to our loyalty, which properly belongs to our perceptions of men and women as the ultimate units of value in our day-to-day view of the world. If we do not thus value the nuclei of consciousness from which all science, all art, all history, all culture, have flowed as symbolic by-products in the humble but intensely urgent business of establishing meaningful relationships between actual human beings, we commit personal suicide. The theology of economics or aesthetics or of any other ordered science of man weighs just as heavily on us, whether we know it or not, as the outmoded theologies of gods and their worshippers. Not for one single moment can we allow ourselves to forget the experienced unity of the individual. No formulations about man and his place in society which do not prove strictly and literally accurate when tested by the experience of the individual can have more than a transitory or technical authority. Hence we need never fear to modify, prune, extend, redefine, rearrange, and reorient our sciences of man as social being, for these sciences cannot point to an order of nature that has meaning apart from the directly experienced perceptions and values of the individual.

"Economic Man"

Let us consider the meaning of the problem of "earning a living." It is not a simple problem, though it is relatively so for the economist. If the economist hears that A gets a salary of $1500.00 a year, his scientific curiosity does not go much beyond trying to ascertain if this income is a normal one for the services that A is said to be rendering. Should he discover that A is a "full professor" at a "university," he will note the fact that the salary is well below the average fee paid in America for the kind of work that "full professors" do. Beyond such observation he will have nothing to offer, though, if he is himself a professor or the son of a professor, he may allow himself a twinge of concern at the imperilment of the economic status of a peculiarly valuable class of person in the cultural scene of contemporary America. But, strictly speaking, A's salary of $1500.00 a year must be interpreted as an item in the strictly economic process of balancing the demand for such services as A is rendering, or is supposed to be rendering, with the supply of individuals capable of rendering them at as low a figure as A is willing to accept. It will not be important for the economist to try to find out if A's salary is as low as it is because he is a member of a poor religious sect which is not in a position to pay more for the full professors of its sectarian university or universities (such curiosity is as unseemly for an economist as would be the desire of a physicist to know whether his falling body was blue or bright red, though the economist might allow his less austere colleague, the sociologist, to indulge in a few musings on the subject) or because A is, as a matter of fact, a millionaire with an educational hobby which he feels he ought to give his fellow citizens the benefit of at small cost to "society." You can't get any more of a personality sketch of A out of the economist than that A just does happen to illustrate a somewhat unusual equilibration of the law of supply and demand.

In fairness to the economist it must be stated that just as he fails to be seriously perturbed over the singularly low economic standard of A, *qua* full professor, so he fails to be greatly saddened by the spectacle of B's efforts to get along on $500.00 a year, even if it can be proved that B is married, has three or four children, and is not a millionaire in disguise. Should B also prove to be a full professor, the

economist might be pardoned if there grows up in
him a more serious uneasiness as to the imperilment
of the economic status of a class in which, being
a member of it, he has after all a little more than a
merely mathematical interest. But no, B is not a
full professor, he is merely a farmer and the economist is quickly reassured that all's well with B, or,
if B really is having a desperately hard time of it,
at least all's well with B *qua* farmer, for he finds
that B's income is snugly within the normal limits
of income earned by American agriculturists—among
the most useful of our various classes of citizens, he
is quite willing to add. Here too the economist is
very skillful in placing B at any one of those strategic corners of space and time in which certain factors of supply and demand get properly equilibrated.
Anyway, if his irrelevant "personalistic," not to say
humanitarian, interests are too greatly aroused, he
can take quick comfort in the fact that the average
income of the American farmer is well above $500.00
a year, so that B, a member of the farmer class,
ought not to be too greatly discouraged. Or, if B
is not easily reassured, at least those who tend to be
worried about B should cease to be so. Of course
B may be a peculiarly shiftless person, but the economist will not press that point. It is better to be sta-
tistically magnanimous and to content oneself with
reflecting that B just does happen to stand at one
of the less rewarding corners of space and time.
There is no need to develop an essentially "unscientific" interest in B's personality, in his "cultural" background, and in the nature of the value judgments

and "symbolisms" of society re B that add up to so trifling an emolument for this particular farmer.

In still further fairness to the economist it should be said that not only is he prepared to accept as "normal" or "natural" incomes that an ordinary person or even a sociologist might describe as "subnormal" or "unnatural," from an angle of observation that subtends much more than the field of operation of "economic laws," but he is also prepared to accept as entirely "normal" or "natural" incomes that are fantastically beyond the ability of anyone to "handle" except by way of the most peculiar, remote, picturesque, symbolic, in short, dream-like or make-believe, extensions of the personalities of the recipients of such incomes. Should any impertinent, thoroughly unscientific, snooper whisper to the economist that, so far as he can see, C's $500,000.00 income (in virtue of his vice-presidency of the X bank plus shareholdership in the Y company plus investment in the Z oil-fields of Mexico plus a long list of other services rendered his fellowmen) seems to be strangely unaffected by the tissue of physical and psychological performances of the psycho-physical entity or organism called C, it making apparently little difference whether C is on hand to instruct one of his secretaries to cut his coupons or is resting up in the Riviera, the economist loses patience. If he then speaks at all, it is to point out that, regardless of C's to him unknown and forever unknowable personality, C does, as a matter of fact, render just such services as society demands and receives just such emoluments as society is "agreed" naturally flow from the rendering of these services and that the supposed "facts" about C are of no more interest to him than are, to a professor of alphabetology, certain reports about bad boys scrawling obscene words on a brick wall instead of turning out Shakespearian plays.

In desperation, then, let us admit that the economist is right and reflect, once and for all, that the economist is no more interested in human beings than the alphabetologist is interested in literature, the numismatist in the morality of the kings of Bactria, or the theologian in the chemical rationalization of miracles; that is to say, respectively, *qua* economist, *qua* alphabetologist, *qua* numismatist, *qua* theologian. These various scientists have their "universes of discourse" that they are extremely proud of, through the instrumentality of which they secure valuable definitions of their egos and at least partially earn their living, and there's an end of it. The necessarily fragmentary, philosophically arbitrary "universe of discourse" gets provided with an excellent terminology, more or less self-contained and self-consistent principles, and some insight, however tangential, into a highly selective phase of human behavior (including human opinion about divine behavior).

There is no mischief in all this, once it is clearly understood that the scientist of man has chief concern for science, not for man, and that all science, partly for better and partly for worse, has the self-feeding voracity of an obsessive ritual. We must give up our naïve faith in the ability of the scientist to tell us anything about man that is not expressible in terms of the verbal definitions and operations that prevail in his "universe of discourse"—a beautiful, dream-like domain that has fitful reminiscences of man as an experiencing organism but is not, and cannot be, immersed in the wholeness of that experience. Hence, while economics can tell us much about the technical operations that prevail in the conceptually well-defined "economic field," a specific type of "universe of discourse" which has only fragmentary and, at many points, even a fictional relation to the universe of experienced behavior, it cannot give us a working conception of *man* even in his abstracted role of earning a living, for the experiential implications of earning a living are not seen by the economist as part of his scientific concern.

MAN AS MAN

But it is precisely these experiential implications that we non-economists are interested in. We want to know what making a living (just about making it or failing to make it or making it a hundred times over) does to A and B and C. To what extent is the specific economic functioning of A and B and C of importance, not only to themselves and those immediately dependent on them, but to all human beings who come in contact with them and, beyond these empirical kinds of importance, to the eye of science? Not, to be sure, to the eye of any safely ticketed science that has its conceptual vested interests to conserve but to an inclusive science of man, one that does the best it can to harbor the value judgments of experiencing human beings within its own catholic "universe of discourse." Such a science will perhaps be called a dangerous or treacherous congeries of opinions, ranging all the way from the feeble aspirations of theologically or classically tinctured humanism to the sentimental, direct-action interferences of mental hygiene. But we need not be so pessimistic. For centuries the only escape from fragmentarism was into the too ambitious dream-worlds of philosophy, worlds defined by the assumption that the human intelligence could behold the universe instead of twinkling within. Now that philosophy is being progressively redefined as a highly technical critique of the validity or conditionality of judgments, it is interesting to see two disciplines—each of them highly apologetic about its scientific credentials—which are taking on the character of inclusive perception of human events and personal relations in as powerfully conceptualized form as possible. These condensations of human experience are cultural anthropology and psychiatry—both of them poorly chosen terms, but we can do no better for the moment.

CULTURAL ANTHROPOLOGY AND PSYCHIATRY

Each of these disciplines has its special "universe of discourse" but at least this universe is so broadly conceived that, under favorable circumstances, either of them can take on the character of a true science of man. Through the sheer weight of cultural detail and, more than that, through the far-reaching personality-conditioning implications of variations in the forms of socialized behavior, the cultural anthropologist may, if he chooses, advance from his relatively technical problems of cultural definition, distribution, organization, and history to more intimate problems of cultural meaning, both for individuals and for significantly definable groups of individuals. And the psychiatrist may, if he chooses, advance from theories of personality disorganization to theories of personality organization, which, in the long run, have little meaning unless they are buttressed by a comprehension of the cultural setting in which the individual ceaselessly struggles to express himself. The anthropologist, in other words, needs only to trespass a little on the untilled acres of psychology, the psychiatrist to poach a few of the uneaten apples of anthropology's Golden Bough.

So far the great majority of both kinds of scientists —if that proud classification be granted them—have feared to advance very far into the larger fields that lie open before them, and for a good reason. The fear of losing the insignia of standing in their respective disciplines, still dangerously insecure in the hierarchy of science, leads to an anxious snobbery which is easily misunderstood as modesty or self-restraint. But at least they have this great advantage, so far as the study of man is concerned: neither, in his heart of hearts, believes that the economist or the political scientist or the aesthetician or any other sort of technical expert in conceptually isolated realms or aspects of man's behavior is in a position to talk real sense about that behavior. An anthropologist knows that you can't talk economics without talking about religion or superstition at the same time; the psychiatrist

knows that you can't talk economics without drop-
ping some rather important hints about mental health
and disease. On the whole, it seems safest to keep
such knowledge in one's heart of hearts and to act
as though one were content to carry on from where
the economist left off. Therefore, as culturalists, let
us not be too much concerned with what sorts of cultural universes A and B and C are living in; as psychiatrists, let us not be too much concerned with
what the play of "economic forces" is doing to A and
B and C and be satisfied to mumble, as occasion
arises, something quite discreet about how an income
of $500.00 a year would not seem to discourage B's
paranoid trends or about how poor C's Don Juanism,
with its secret unhappiness, might possibly have been
mitigated if he had only had an income of $5000.00
a year to play with. It is so easy to be paranoid on
$500.00 a year and it is so difficult to be a Don Juan
—and C, by the way, is not an Apollo—on $500.00
a year.

Economic Factors in Personal Adjustment

Everybody really knows a good deal about what
economics has to do with the personal distribution
of "cultural patterns" and with mental health. The
facts are pitifully obvious. Professors who earn
only $1500.00 a year cannot go to the opera very
often and must therefore go in for plain living and
high thinking. If they have good health, are happily
married, and have more than average intelligence,
they and their wives can manage to stave off envy
of the banker and real-estate agent and their re-

spective wives, mingle sturdy Puritanism with a sub-
scription to "The Nation," and construct a pretty
good cultural world for themselves. After all,
$1500.00 is three times as much as $500.00 But if their
health is not too good, if they are not too happily
married, and if their intelligence, as generally proves
to be the case, is about average, then it is to be
feared that $1500.00 is not quite sufficient to buy
themselves enough of cultural participation to stave
off that corroding envy of the banker and real-estate
agent and their respective wives which, psychiatrists
tell us, is not very good for either the digestive tract
or the personality organization. So, one surmises, a
salary of $1500.00 a year for a full professor may have
a good deal to do with the gradual cultural impoverishment of A's universe. A normal vitality will mask
the degenerative cultural and psychiatric process
from himself, his neighbors, the trustees of the university and, above all, the economist, who, having
been unpleasantly jarred for a moment by his threat
to the salary curve of full professors, need never think
of him again.

At first A's difficulties find their solution in a
slightly apologetic vein of irony, which cultivated
visitors find rather charming. A certain school of social psychologists might at this point even prove that
A was quite appreciably enriching culture both for
himself and society. (Few would have the hardihood
to suggest that he was enriching the cultural world
of his wife, though his children might be robust
enough to pick up a few crumbs of value or, perhaps, more accurately, a few ambivalently colored

experiences which the softening retrospect of later years will transmute into crumbs of value—if not indeed into a philosophy, so strong is the magic of Illusion.) But A's charm does not wear well, no better than the loveliness, once so fashionable, of the incipiently tubercular flush. Any competent novelist may step in at this point and tell us about the fascinating story of his growing sense of isolation, his growing morbidity, the growing concern of the trustees of the university for the mental health of his students, his inevitable, though regrettable, dismissal, and of how, in sheer desperation, he founded a new religion (it was a sectarian university after all), gave Robinson Jeffers a chance to write a masterpiece (which the economist's wife, if not the economist, can read with comfortable gusto), thereby again adding materially, though in a more passive sense, to America's store of cultural values, when, apparently out of a blue sky, his wife, unable to determine whether she loved him or hated him, committed suicide. Apparently the equilibrating power of $1500.00 a year was not enough to avert the tragedy. Dare either the culturalist or the psychiatrist say that a salary raise of $500.00 would have had no cultural or psychiatric importance? The feeble vein of irony might have grown into a sturdy fortress, for with an extra $500.00 he could have just managed to buy his wife a dress barely good enough to have them go to the annual tea given by the banker (we forgot to say that he was one of the trustees of the university) for the express purpose of having faculty and trustees get to know each other. As it is, he was morbidly isolated, she no less. And, if the truth were known, Robinson Jeffers had a lot of other things to write about.

All of this, the economist insists—and quite rightly —is neither here nor there. If sociologists want to worry about such things, let them. They don't have to be so scientific. But most sociologists dearly wish to be scientific. They collect case histories, to be sure, but it is generally seen to that they contain just enough data to make it possible to discover general truths (such as that full professors in southern universities are less amply rewarded for their services than in northern universities) but not enough data to make A intelligible. That would be invading the field of the novelist and no scientist, *qua* scientist, can afford to do that. So we must turn to the psychiatrist, it seems, and ask him to be so kind as to add the following law or observation or principle (the exact terminological placement of this truth to be decided on later): "Whoever is sophisticated enough, sensitive enough and representative enough of our country's higher culture to get himself appointed a full professor in one of the universities of said country, cannot, if he is married, be expected, in view of the known cost of many requisite symbols of status, to be either happy or comfortable at a salary which is less than a quarter (the figure is merely a random suggestion) of the income of the averagely prosperous banker or real-estate agent of the community in which he lives, it being presumed that the remaining three-quarters (or other suitable figure) be more or less adequately compensated for by such substitutive values as membership in scientific societies and the habit of reading difficult but not too expensive literature. It is suggested that $1500.00 a year is well below the safe minimum for such a person. In the absence of powerful personality-preserving factors, such as unusually robust health or a far more than averagely happy marriage, so low a salary must be considered a definite factor in the possible deterioration of the professor's personality."

If the psychiatrist exclaims that this is mixing psychiatry and economics with a vengeance, we must gently remind him that personalities live in tangible environments and that the business of making a living is one of the bed-rock factors in their environmental adjustment. We are not in a position to distinguish sharply between innate or organismal strains, physical and psychological, and so-called external strains. They come to us fatally blended in practice and it is a wise man who can presume to say which is of more decisive importance. For all practical purposes a too low income is at least as significant a datum in the causation of mental ill-health as a buried Oedipus complex or sex trauma. Why should not the psychiatrist be frank enough to call attention to the great evils of unemployment or of lack of economic security? His recognized concern for the well-being of the individual gives him every right to be heard, where ordinary opinion or common sense is often dismissed as governed by sentimental prejudices.

Now as to the starveling farmer and his $500.00 income, he is too busy, from dawn to bed-time, to know whether his health is good or bad and he hasn't the faintest notion whether he is happily married or not. Imperious task follows task in an all-day grind, he barely manages, he cannot pay off his mortgage, he is thankful for reprieves. The notion of mental ill-health is a luxury to him, he'd rather suspect himself of laziness—there's so much to be done—just as he'd rather suspect the other fellow of being a little weak in the head than waste breath on the ill-effects of extreme poverty. His class comes in relatively little contact with the psychiatrist and the mental hygienist. You either somehow manage or you "bust." If you manage, there's little need to graduate the psychological quality of the performance. Happiness, soul-weariness, apathy, envy, petty greed, are just so many novelistic fancies, utterly dwarfed by the solid facts that the potatoes didn't do so well this year, that the cows must be milked as usual, that the market for hay is unexpectedly poor. It is only when the sober, inevitable, corroding impoverishment of the farmer's personality is lit up by some spectacular morbidity of sex or religion that the psychiatrist or novelist or poet is attracted to him. The far more important dullness of daily routine, of futile striving, of ceaseless mental thwarting, does not seem to clamor for the psychiatrist's analysis.

All this is known to be "uninteresting," hence we prettify the facts as best we can with shreds of folklore, survivals of a pioneering culture that had a self-containedness and satisfyingness of its own. That culture has rotted away and our farmer is little more than a disgruntled economic drudge and a cultural parasite. It is not only worth the psychiatrist's while to inquire into these conditions and report on them, it is his duty to do so. Perhaps we could better understand morbid religious frenzies, lynch law, and other devastating phenomena of contemporary American life if we looked more closely into the psychological tissue of our rural life. "North of Boston" and Faulkner's exhibits need to be supplemented by the sober case history and by the economico-psychiatric appraisal of the conditions of life in our rural sections.

As to C, the interest of the psychiatrist in his moods, conflicts, and aspirations is perennial. He has his troubles, it seems, his surfeits and futilities, and we are all glad to know that the psychiatrist is eager to put his technical skill at his disposal. All human life is sacred—to hark back to a nineteenth century prejudice—and C should, most certainly, be made a happier man, if C will only let the psychiatrist define happiness, which I take to be a synonym of mental health, for him. But is it wrong to remark that for every suffering C there are many thousands of suffering A's and many thousands of suffering B's? We shall not try to fantasy what ails C, there are many admirable textbooks of psychiatry which give us a fair notion of how to be miserable though wealthy. Perhaps C too inclines to suffer from an economic ill —that obscure, perverse, guilt feeling which, the psychiatrist tells us, so often festers in one's heart of hearts when one tries to balance one's usefulness to society with the size of one's income. Here too is a chance for psychiatrists to be reasonably vocal. Is it conceivable that good mental hygiene, even expert psychiatry, may find it proper to recommend some share of income reduction for the sake of the mental health of those who are too heavily burdened by a material prosperity that far outruns their needs or, if the truth were known, their secret desires? In this mysterious realm we need further light.

The Emergence of the Concept of Personality in a Study of Cultures

Our natural interest in human behavior seems always to vacillate between what is imputed to the culture of the group as a whole and what is imputed to the psychic organization of the individual himself. These two poles of our interest in behavior do not necessarily make use of different materials; it is merely that the locus of reference is different in the two cases. Under familiar circumstances and with familiar people, the locus of reference of our interest is likely to be the individual. In unfamiliar types of behavior, such as running a dynamo, or with individuals who do not readily fit into the normal contexts of social habit, say a visiting Chinese mandarin, the interest tends to discharge itself into formulations which are cultural rather than personal in character. If I see my little son playing marbles I do not, as a rule, wish to have light thrown on how the game is played. Nearly everything that I observe tends to be interpreted as a contribution to the understanding of the child's personality. He is bold or timid, alert or easily confused, a good sport or a bad sport when he loses, and

Journal of Social Psychology, vol. 5 (1934), 408–415. Based on a paper presented to the National Research Council Conference on Studies in Child Development at Chicago on June 22, 1933.

so on. The game of marbles, in short, is merely an excuse, as it were, for the unfolding of various facts or theories about a particular individual's psychic constitution. But when I see a skilled laborer oiling a dynamo, or a polished mandarin seating himself at the dinner table in the capacity of academic guest, it is almost inevitable that my observations take the form of ethnographic field notes, the net result of which is likely to be facts or theories about such cultural patterns as the running of a dynamo or Chinese manners.

Ordinarily one's interest is not so sharply defined. It tingles with both personal and cultural implications. There is no awareness of the constantly shifting direction of interest. Moreover, there is much of that confusion which attends all experience in its initial stages in childhood, when the significant personality is interpreted as an institution and every cultural pattern is merely a memory of what this or that person has actually done. Now and then, it is true, there arises in the flow of adult experience a certain intuition of what would be the significant eventual formulation, personal or cultural, of a given fragment of behavior. "Yes, that is just like John," or "But we mustn't make too much of this trifle. Presumably all Chinamen do the same thing under the circumstances"; are illustrative symbols for contrasting interpretations. Naturally the confusion of interests is one not merely of the mingling of directions but also of an actual transposition or inversion. A stubbornly individual variation may be misinterpreted as a cultural datum. This sort of thing is likely to happen when we learn a foreign language from a single individual and are not in a position to distinguish between what is characteristic of the language and what is peculiar to the teacher's speech. More often, perhaps, the cultural pattern, when significantly presented in experience, tends to allocate to itself a far too intimate meaning. Qualities of charm or quaintness for instance, are notoriously dangerous in this regard and tend to be not so much personal as cultural data, which receive their especial contextual value from the inability of the observer to withhold a strictly personal interpretation.

What is the genesis of our duality of interest in the facts of behavior? Why is it necessary to discover the contrast, real or fictitious, between culture and personality, or, to speak more accurately, between a segment of behavior seen as cultural pattern and a segment of behavior interpreted as having a person-defining value? Why cannot our interest in behavior maintain the undifferentiated character which it possessed in early childhood? The answer, presumably, is that each type of interest is necessary for the psychic preservation of the individual in an environment which experience makes increasingly complex and unassimilable on its own simple terms. The interests connected by the terms culture and personality are necessary for intelligent and helpful growth because each is based on a distinctive kind of imaginative participation by the observer in the life around him. The observer may dramatize such behavior as he takes note of in terms of a set of values, a conscience which is beyond self and to which he must conform, actually or imaginatively, if he is to preserve his place in the world of authority or impersonal social necessity. Or, on the other hand, he may feel the behavior as self-expressive, as defining the reality of individual consciousness against the mass of environing social determinants. Observations coming within the framework of the former of these two kinds of participation constitute our knowledge of culture. Those which come within the framework of the latter constitute our knowledge of personality. One is as subjective or objective as the other, for both are essentially modes of projection of personal experience into the analysis of social phenomena. Culture may be psychoanalytically reinterpreted as the supposedly impersonal aspect of those values and definitions which come to the child with the irresistible authority of the father, mother, or other individuals of their class. The child does not feel itself to be contributing to culture through his personal interaction but is the passive recipient of values which lie completely beyond his control and which have a necessity and excellence that he dare not question. We may therefore venture to surmise that one's earliest configurations of experience have more of the character of what is later to be rationalized as culture than of what the psychologist is likely to abstract as personality. We have all had the disillusioning experience of revising our father and mother images down from the institutional plane to the purely personal one. The discovery of the world of personality is apparently dependent upon the ability of the individual to become aware of and to attach value to his resistance to authority. It could probably be shown that naturally conservative people find it difficult to take personality valuations seriously, while temperamental radicals tend to be impatient with a purely cultural analysis of human behavior.

It may be questioned whether a dichotomy which seems to depend so largely on the direction of one's interest in observed behavior can be an altogether safe guide to the study of behavior in social situations. The motivations of these contrasting directions of interest are unconscious, to be sure, yet simple enough, as all profound motivations must be. The study of culture as such, which may be called sociology or anthropology, has a deep and unacknowledged root in the desire to lose oneself safely in the historically determined patterns of behavior. The motive for the study of personality, which we may term indifferently social psychology or psychiatry, proceeds from the necessity which the ego feels to assert itself significantly. Both the cultural disciplines and the psychological disciplines are careful to maintain objective ideals, but it should not be difficult to see that neither the cultural pattern as such nor the personality as such, abstracted as both of these are from the directly given facts of experience, can, in the long run, escape from the peculiarly subtle subjectivism which is implicit in the definitions of the disciplines themselves. As preliminary disciplines, whose main purpose is to amass and critically sift data and help us to phrase significant problems of human behavior, they are of course invaluable. But sooner or later their obscure opposition of spirit must be transcended for an objectivity which is not merely formal and non-evaluative but which boldly essays to bring every cultural pattern back to the living context from which it has been abstracted in the first place and, in parallel fashion, to bring every fact of personality formation back to its social matrix. The problems herewith suggested are, of course, neither simple nor easy. The social psychology into which the conventional cultural and psychological disciplines must eventually be resolved is related to these paradigmatic studies as an investigation into living speech is related to grammar. I think few cultural disciplines are as exact, as rigorously configurated, as self-contained as grammar, but if it is desired to have grammar contribute a significant share to our understanding of human behavior, its definitions, meanings, and classifications must be capable of a significant restatement in terms of a social psychology which transcends the best that we have yet been able to offer in this perilous field of investigation. What applies to grammar applies no less significantly, of course, to the study of social organization, religion, art, mythology, technology, or any segment, large or small, or groups of segments which convenience or tradition leads us to carve out of the actual contexts of human behavior.

There is a very real hurt done our understanding of culture when we systematically ignore the individual and his types of interrelationship with other individuals. It is no exaggeration to say that cultural analysis as ordinarily made is not a study of behavior at all but is essentially the orderly description, without evaluation, or, at best, with certain implicit evaluations, of a behavior to be hereinafter defined but which, in the normal case is not, perhaps cannot be, defined. Culture, as it is ordinarily constructed by the anthropologist, is a more or less mechanical sum of the more striking or picturesque generalized patterns of behavior which he has either abstracted for himself out of the sum total of his observations or has had abstracted for him by his informants in verbal communication. Such a "culture," because generally constructed of unfamiliar terms, has an almost unavoidable picturesqueness about it, which suggests a vitality which it does not, as a matter of scrupulous psychological fact, embody. The cultures so carefully described in our ethnological and sociological monographs are not, and cannot be, the truly objective entities they claim to be. No matter how accurate their individual itemization, their integrations into suggested structures are uniformly fallacious and unreal. This cannot be helped so long as we confine ourselves to the procedures recognized as sound by orthodox ethnology. If we make the test of imputing the contents of an ethnological monograph to a known individual in the community which it describes, we would inevitably be led to discover that, while every single statement in it may, in the favorable case, be recognized as holding true in some sense, the complex of patterns as described cannot, without considerable absurdity, be interpreted as a significant configuration of experience, both actual and potential, in the life of the person appealed to. Cultures, as ordinarily dealt with, are merely abstracted configura-

tions of idea and action patterns, which have end-
lessly different meanings for the various individuals
in the group and which, if they are to build up into
any kind of significant psychic structure, whether for
the individual or the small group or the larger group,
must be set in relation to each other in a complex
configuration of evaluations, inclusive and exclusive
implications, priorities, and potentialities of realization which cannot be discovered from an inquiry into
the described patterns.

The more fully one tries to understand a culture,
the more it seems to take on the characteristics of a
personality organization. Patterns first present themselves according to a purely formalized and logically
developed scheme. More careful explorations invariably reveal the fact that numerous threads of symbolism or implication connect patterns or parts of
patterns with others of an entirely different formal
aspect. Behind the simple diagrammatic forms of culture is concealed a peculiar network of relationships,
which, in their totality, carve out entirely new forms
that stand in no simple relation to the obvious cultural table of contents. Thus, a word, a gesture, a
genealogy, a type of religious belief may unexpectedly join hands in a common symbolism of status
definition. If it were the aim of the study of culture
merely to list and describe comprehensively the vast
number of supposedly self-contained patterns of behavior which are handed on from generation to generation by social processes, such an inquiry as we
have suggested into the more intimate structure of
culture would hardly be necessary. Trouble arises

only when the formulations of the culture student are requisitioned without revision or criticism for an understanding of the most significant aspects of human behavior. When this is done, insoluble difficulties necessarily appear, for behavior is not a recomposition of abstracted patterns, each of which can be more or less successfully studied as a historically continuous and geographically distributed entity in itself, but the very matrix out of which the abstractions have been made in the first place. All this means, of course, that if we are justified in speaking of the growth of culture at all, it must be in the spirit, not of a composite history made up of the private histories of particular patterns, but in the spirit of the development of a personality. The complete, impersonalized "culture" of the anthropologist can really be little more than an assembly or mass of loosely overlapping idea and action systems which, through verbal habit, can be made to assume the appearance of a closed system of behavior. What tends to be forgotten is that the functioning of such a system, if it can be said to have any ascertainable function at all, is due to the specific functioning and interplays of the idea and action systems which have actually grown up in the minds of given individuals. In spite of the often assorted impersonality of culture, the humble truth remains that vast reaches of culture, far from being in any real sense "carried" by a community or a group as such, are discoverable only as the peculiar property of certain individuals, who cannot but give these cultural goods the impress of their own personality. With the disappearance of such key individuals, the tight, "objectified" culture loosens up at once and is eventually seen to be a convenient fiction of thought.

When the cultural anthropologist has finished his necessary preliminary researches into the overt forms of culture and has gained from them an objectivity of reference by working out their forms, time sequences, and geographical distribution, there emerges for him the more difficult and significant task of interpreting the culture which he has isolated in terms of its relevance for the understanding of the personalities of the very individuals from whom he has obtained his information. As he changes his informant, his culture necessarily changes. There is no reason why the culturalist should be afraid of the concept of personality, which must not, however, be thought of, as one inevitably does at the beginning of his thinking, as a mysterious entity resisting the historically given culture but rather as a distinctive configuration of experience which tends always to form a psychologically significant unit and which, as it accretes more and more symbols to itself, creates finally that cultural microcosm of which official "culture" is little more than a metaphorically and mechanically expanded copy. The application of the point of view which is natural in the study of the genesis of personality to the problem of culture cannot but force a revaluation of the materials of culture itself. Many problems which are now in the forefront of investigation sink into a secondary position, and patterns of behavior which seem so obvious or universal as not to be worthy of the distinctive attention of the ethnologist leap into a new and unexpected importance. The ethnologist may some day have to face the uncomfortable predicament of inquiring into such humble facts as whether the father is in the habit of acting as indulgent guide or as disciplinarian to his son and of regarding the problem of the child's membership inside or outside of his father's clan as a relatively subsidiary question. In short, the application of the personality point of view tends to minimize the bizarre or exotic in alien cultures and to reveal to us more and more clearly the broad human base on which all culture has developed. The profound commonplace that all culture starts from the needs of a common humanity is believed in by all anthropologists, but it is not demonstrated by their writings.

An excellent test of the fruitfulness of the study of culture in close conjunction with a study of personality would be provided by studies in the field of child development. It is strange how little ethnology has concerned itself with the intimate genetic problem of the acquirement of culture by the child. In the current language of ethnology culture dynamics seems to be almost entirely a matter of adult definition and adult transmission from generation to generation and from group to group. The humble child, who is laboriously orienting himself in the world of his society, yet is not, in the normal case, sacrificing his forthright psychological status as a significant ego, is somehow left out of account. This strange omission is obviously due to the fact that anthropology has allowed itself to be victimized by a convenient but dangerous metaphor. This metaphor is always persuading us that culture is a neatly packed up assemblage of forms of behavior handed over piecemeal, but without serious breakage, to the passively inquiring child. I have come to feel that it is precisely the supposed "givenness" of culture that is the most serious obstacle to our real understanding of the nature of culture and cultural change and of their relationship to individual personality. Culture is not, as a matter of sober fact, a "given" at all. It is so only by a polite convention of speech. As soon as we set ourselves at the vantage point of the culture-acquiring child, the personality definitions and potentials that must never for a moment be lost sight of, and which are destined from the very beginning to interpret, evaluate, and modify every culture pattern, sub-pattern, or assemblage of patterns that it will ever be influenced by, everything changes. Culture is then not something given but something to be gradually and gropingly discovered. We then see at once that elements of culture that come well within the horizon of awareness of one individual are entirely absent in another individual's landscape. This is an important fact, systematically ignored by the cultural anthropologist. It may be proper for the systematic ethnologist to ignore such pattern differences as these, but for the theoretical anthropologist, who wishes to place culture in a general view of human behavior, such an oversight is inexcusable. Furthermore, it is obvious that the child will unconsciously accept the various elements of culture with entirely different meanings, according to the biographical conditions that attend their introduction to him. It may, and un-doubtedly does, make a profound difference whether a religious ritual comes with the sternness of the father's authority or with the somewhat playful indul-gence of the mother's brother. We have not the privi-lege of assuming that it is an irrelevant matter how musical stimuli are introduced to the child. The fact that the older brother is already an admired pianist in the little household may act as an effective barrier to the development of interest in any form of musical expression. Such a child may grow up curiously ob-tuse to musical values and may be persuaded to think that he was born with a naturally poor ear and is therefore debarred from sharing in the blessings of one important aspect of the cultural life of the com-munity.

If we take the purely genetic point of view, all the problems which appear in the study of culture reap-pear with a startling freshness which cannot but mean much for the rephrasing of these problems. Problems of symbolism, of superordination and subordination of patterns, of relative strength of emotional character, of transformability and transmis-sibility, of the isolability of certain patterns into rela-tively closed systems, and numerous others of like dynamic nature, emerge at once. We cannot answer any of them in the abstract. All of them demand pa-tient investigation and the answers are almost cer-tain to be multiform. We may suggest as a difficult but crucial problem of investigation the following: Study the child minutely and carefully from birth until, say the age of ten with a view to seeing the order in which cultural patterns and parts of patterns appear in his psychic world; study the relevance of these patterns for the development of his personality; and, at the end of the suggested period, see how much of the total official culture of the group can be said to have a significant existence for him. Moreover, what degree of systematization, conscious or unconscious, in the complicating patterns and symbolisms of culture will have been reached by this child? This is a difficult problem, to be sure, but it is not an impossible one. Sooner or later it will have to be attacked by the genetic psychologists. I venture to predict that the concept of culture which will then emerge, fragmentary and confused as it will undoubtedly be, will turn out to have a tougher, more vital, importance for social thinking than the tidy tables of contents attached to this or that group which we have been in the habit of calling "cultures."